MY TALK – BOOK FIVE

This picture was taken from the internet and the Jamaica Observer owns the copyright to this photo. Man I miss the days of going to the river to wash mi dirty clothes dem. Wow. Truly thank you Jamaica Observer for bringing back some wonderful memories of days past.

Jamaica mi waane cry fi yu again but I have to let my tears stay. How the island and people are running thing is truly not right. Look at the beautiful island Good God has and have given you and seaka greed unnu condemn di island! Laade mi grieve to know sey, WHEY GOOD GOD GI WI WI NUH WANT EEE. HENCE OLE PEOPLE SEY, WANTI WANTI CAANE GET EEE, AN GETTI GETTI NUH WANT EEE. This is so sad, but this is our reality. Laade look at the beautiful land and name yu gi wi an wi mash up di lan. Ja, no other nation on the face of this planet can boast the name of God – Good God and Allelujah an unnu get im name and dash eee wey suh. Good things none of you wanted; hence JamaicaF. Jamaica (Good God) gaane from wi literally. **Wow; amazing, and we say we are Africans and truly do not know we had the true Africa because GOOD GOD NEVER LEFT US; HE RESIDES IN US LITERALLY.**

MICHELLE JEAN

In all I think, I think of you.

I think of what it would be like to fully and truly know you; have you.

I think of what it would be like without you.
Think of what it would be like to be truly spoiled by you.
You are my hope and dreams
Trust
Total desire
Truth

But with all this said; I am missing something; truly missing you. I know you are trying to tell me something but what? What are you trying to tell me and what am I missing? Yes I've journeyed to another phase in life and it's different because now I am at the White Level; The White Level of life and things are certainly different because this level entails water and all White People.

Wow because it's April 17, 2015 and the conversation came up about WHITES BEING THE SUPERIOR RACE based on hue. Now me being me, in my dream had to put my two cents in but no one was listening; **WHITE PEOPLE DID NOT WANT TO HEAR THE TRUTH.** To them whites are superior to blacks and this is a crying shame. But it matters not to me what they think, because in the dream I put them in their place. **There is no**

superiority of race when it comes to skin tone. OUR SKIN TONE AS HUMANS REPRESENT DEATH, THE WAY WE DIE. SO NO MATTER HOW YOU LOOK AT IT; DEATH IS NOT SUPERIOR TO DEATH. No I should not say this, because when **I SEE A WHITE PERSON I SEE DEATH, SPIRITUAL DEATH.** *This is the way everyone dies in the spiritual realm, so death cannot change ever,* **DEATH MUST ALWAYS STAY WHITE; THE SAME.** *Yes hence White Jesus dressing in white. So when you base life off hue; all I will do now is laugh and call you an idiot because you as WHITES KNOW NOT THE TRUTH, NOR DO YOU KNOW YOUR TRUE HISTORY AND OR LINEAGE.*

To break free from this, I was watching this show on the internet which had to do with Albinism. Now this white woman was saying people with Albinism have a genetically inherited disorder. **She also called Albinism a disease.** *(Xakhubasa: The White Pride)*

Now when she said, **Albinism is a disease that truly pissed me the hell off.** *But then again nothing should surprise me when it comes to White South Africans.* And yes I am assuming she's White South African. No Fam, I am pissed. Who the hell is she to call Albinism a disease? **DID SHE TAKE A LOOK AT HER SKIN?** SO IF PEOPLE WITH ALBINISM IS A DISEASE AND OR HAVE A DISEASE, THEN WHAT THE BLEEP IS SHE? **IS SHE NOT A DAMNED DISEASE ALSO?** SHE LACKS PIGMENTATION OF THE SKIN. SHE IS WHITE AND LACKS A CERTAIN AMOUNT OF MELANIN ALSO. So don't class people as a disease if you of yourself don't want to be classed. Humanity knows not the extent of the genes. Humans categorize people and things without knowing the full truth. **SO HUMANITY CAN SAY THE WHITE RACE IS A CURSE BECAUSE THEY ARE THE ONES TO BRING ABOUT DISEASES.**

HUMANITY CAN SAY THE WHITE RACE IS A WALKING, BREATHING, TALKING AND STINKING DISEASE FACTORY BECAUSE EVERYWHERE THEY GO THEY BRING THEIR DISEASES WITH THEM AND POLLUTE THE AIR AND ENVIRONMENT THAT PEOPLE LIVE IN.

So truly do not class someone and or a race of people as a disease because none in the white race is better than anyone. YOUR RACE WHICH IS THE

SICK RACE RESIDES ALONE ON THE MOUNTAIN OF GOOD GOD AND ALLELUJAH. YOUR RACE CARRY SICKNESS – THE SICKNESS GENE OR GENES. NO OTHER RACE WAS WITH YOU OR ON YOUR LEVEL OF THE MOUNTAIN OF GOOD GOD BECAUSE I DID NOT SEE ONE (ANOTHER RACE) WITH YOU. So truly step off. EVERYONE HAS THE WHITE GENE IN THEM; MEANING BLACK PEOPLE CARRY THE WHITE GENE (S) BECAUSE IT IS FROM THE BLACK MAN'S LOINS THAT THE WHITE RACE CAME FROM. YES THE ENVIRONMENT PLAYS A FACTOR IN THIS AS WELL. So this and or the superiority bullshit trip that some of you White People are on, please stop it. <u>HUMAN LIFE DID NOT ORIGINATE WITH WHITE PEOPLE; IT ORIGINATED WITH BLACKS AND CHINESE. THEY ARE AT THE BASE OF THE MOUNTAIN OF GOOD GOD.</u> **<u>You the white race is at the second level</u>** and yes I can say this is due to sin; a curse but I refuse to say this because it is not right, I know the full truth. Both races carry each other's genes; hence we are from the same GENE POOL THUS ALBINISM IN ANIMALS AND MAN; HUMANS AND NATURE. So stop the superiority bullshit now man come on now. Know this; **none can TAKE COLOUR AND OR HUE TO GOD; GOOD GOD**

AND ALLELUJAH. So your hatred of blacks is not warranted nor is the hatred of whites by blacks warranted. **YOU'RE BOTH THE SAME; BLEEPING DEATH. ONE IS PHYSICAL DEATH AND THE OTHER IS SPIRITUAL DEATH.** So bleep all of you with the hue and or colour of skin bullshit. Know the truth; **HENCE THE YING AND YANG IS THERE TO PULL YA'LL IGNORANT ASSES IN YOUR PLACE.**

Ignorant, ignorant, ignorant thus none of you want to know the truth. You would rather bask in your lies and continue on with your bullshit hatred and racism instead of knowing the truth and live by the truth.

Society makes me so sick that I literally want to vomit at the bullshit many in humanity are fed and spread.

Don't hate because you don't know. **What you don't know you just don't know.** And yes you can blast me because I've cussed out a few people and call some people unclean, filthy and dirty as well as call some of your gods stink.

I will not base anything off the colour of skin. Yes I can but I refuse to because the hue of man is just that, the hue of man. It is bullshit because our skin stinks. It's riddled with bacteria that consumes us at death; when the spirit sheds the flesh. So all of you who hate based on hue; skin tone can **KISS MY NATURAL BROWN ASS.** Go someplace with your hue and or superiority bullshit because you die like anyone else and you're going to burn in hell like anyone else. So bleep off to you hateful warmongers and haters.

Yes it's April 17, 2015 and the mood is different. Also dreamt my sister. Dreamt she had a baby because she cannot have any more children in the living. In the dream she bent over to show me the blood stains on the back of her clothes but she did not have blood stains, she had grass stains on the back of her clothes. We were walking all the while she was doing this. Her baby needed feeding and we walked to the river. I think she said it and not me. She said; **you did not need blood to have a baby.** I think it was me that said I know. But I did tell her, *__if Good God truly loves you, he provides for you; he spoils you.__* Continuing to walk we got to the river; there was a lot of stones in the water. I wanted to sit down but I could not find a proper stone to sit on. Moving a bit I found a stone for me to sit on and my sister used a black sock to wipe the stone off. I had to tell her to stop; I did not want her to dirty the stone anymore. I wanted to sit on a clean stone people not a dirty one. In the river that had clear water had white women in the water. One passed us and said Hi and I replied in kind. The water we were in was where you would go to feed your baby if you were a nursing mother. So because my sister had the baby we had to go to the river to feed the baby. BUT

THE WEIRD PART OF THIS DREAM IS THAT IT WASN'T MY SISTER THAT SAT TO BREAST FEED AND OR NURSE THE BABY, IT WAS ME THAT BREAST FEED THE BABY SO THAT THE BABY COULD EAT AND OR BE FULL. After I fed him (the baby) he was happy and went on his way with my sister.

I have an idea as to what this dream means, but I am going to watch it and see because I am truly not sure.

I do not know what white women in water have to do with me because I am seeing this more and more. I am seeing more White People and I truly don't know if this is the second level of my spirituality. Hence dreaming about white women in water is new and strange to me. Yes I am journeying along but wow, this is weird.

And yes for all of you that are saying I did not complete Book Four of My Talk you are correct. I don't think I am allowed to go back to what I've written. When I am allowed I will let you know.

I so have to find a place real soon. I can't sit and watch anymore because I know massive homelessness comes and I truly do not want or need to get caught up in this money and or economic grab bag that is going to millions homeless and on the streets real soon. The rich is getting richer while the poor is getting poorer. **It seems we work to feed the rich and or line their pockets** and to me this is not fair or right. I don't know

Fam because I know what faces me shortly and it's not pretty. Homelessness is at my doorsteps and I cannot turn this back. I can't think because I am so stressed. You pay so much for rent to have electricity been added to your rent when your lease agreement specifically say; electricity is included in your rent. Now I am being told the landlord can charge you for electricity if he's having financial difficulties. Now I ask you, how can a single parent function and or feed their family on a limited income?

Hence I have to try and find a place for myself and let my older children go. They have to fend for self now because I cannot continue to do it for them. I cannot journey with them anymore because they are of age. Yes I feel it for them because they are going to face hardships. I know this, but I cannot worry about that. Life has been set this way and I cannot change it. I have to do to preserve me whichever way I can. Whatever I can do to help them I will, but right now I truly have to think of me and my health.

Oh man it's April 18, 2015 and the dreams for LA have not stopped.

Why is LA engrained in me that I have to dream about their virtually every night? Life sucks, truly sucks in this way because I am being taunted by this land and I truly don't know why.

Am I missing something when it comes to LA?

<u>Also dreamt I was praying to Good God in regards to not allowing any Babylonian Jew into his new kingdom and world.</u> I was praying and telling him that I did not want them in his kingdom and world. So to the Babylonian Jews of today; truly good luck because I was praying against you. But I would not put any value on this dream because Good God truly doesn't listen to me anyway. It's like I don't exist with my asking (s) of him, so I leave things alone with him. I have to.

As for today, I truly do not feel like writing nor do I truly want to write. It's a nice day outside and later I'll go for a walk and soak up the night air. And yes I did. I went for a walk on the Boardwalk and it was great.

The night breeze was wonderful and I truly loved it. Walking is fun when you have someone beside you that you can talk to and laugh with. Yes I was silly yesterday but you know what, that was the fun side of me. I don't get to be myself (silly) when I want to, so the opportunity arose yesterday and I took it. Yeah Me!!

Michelle

It's April 19, 2015 and the dreams are coming. Dreamt about snow; the environment and I truly loved it. Snow was on the ground and in the trees. I noticed this one particular snow ball in a tree. Fam it was small and the snow was beautiful. Seeing the tiny snow ball I did not want it to fall out of the tree and spoil the beauty of my surroundings. Wow.

Also dreamt about **TRUTH in that truth is a part of the collective of Good God and Allelujah.** If we do not have truth we cannot reach him. I guess this dream and or vision was confirming this for me. **We all know truth is everlasting life and we have to live by the truth if we want to continue living.** Yes I know billions are going to die because of the lie they believe in and do (sins), but this is their choice. They forgot that **TRUTH IS EVERLASTING AND OR ETERNAL LIFE.** They gave up their truth (Life) for death so they must die.

We all know "THE WAGES OF SIN IS DEATH," so if you want to live by sin; then you must and should know that you are going to die.

So for those of you that are living by the truth continue to do so because better comes. Like I said, humanity lost to Satan and or Sin and or Death in 2013. This is the year that Satan and his people feared. Although the Devil and or Satan won over man, **Satan failed when it came to Good God because they did not secure the faith of all of**

humanity. Good God's children are saved, spared. The harvest comes yes, but the harvest is not for Good God's and Allelujah's people, ***it's for the devil's people; children.*** They failed to secure a place for themselves in life so because of this; they must die; go to hell and die.

The wages of sin is death people.

Also dreamt I was arguing with the White Jews (Babylonian Jews). This man who looked like Matthew Lauer who was dressed in Black took me on. We were in this place; an apartment with lots of White People. I was the only black one there and he was talking smack when it came to Judaism – the Black Jews. Trust me I was ready to take him on and I did. **Hence he confirmed twice the Ethiopians were the original Israelites.** No, he did not like to say it, but he did say it. Like I said, where we were was like an apartment and lineage came up. The apartment we were in did not like an apartment. It looked more like a church setting, but the setting did not look like a church it still looked like an apartment, but without the bedrooms and furniture; kitchen. There was this Chinese looking lady who is a mixture of race to me. She looked more Filipino than Chinese. She was with this White man and she was making out with the White Man. I thought that to be disrespectful because they were kissing; French Kissing in a holy place. This was God's Church and they were disrespecting it. I was asked what lineage I was of and I told them Scottish. I asked them what lineage they were and they said Scottish. **But I doubted them when they said they were of Scottish lineage because they were desecrating a holy place by openly kissing in the church; Good God's sanctuary.** I don't know what happened after that, but the Babylonian Jewish Man that looked like Matthew Lauer said something about truth and or money and gifts, but I know it had to do with truth. I cannot remember what he said, but he began to give the people, White Jewish People money. Let me see if I can find the exact note on Google for you to see.

This is the exact image and monetary notes.

This is the money he was giving to his people including daughter that he loved. It's funny his daughter who is young say about 16 or 17 had this black school bag (knapsack) and she opened it and in it was this black mini fridge with and electrical cord for her to plug into an electrical socket. Weird! Am I going to get off this morning on the White Jews for which I call Babylonian Jews?

No, I will not. I truly can't be bothered because <u>**he confirmed what I already know to be the truth.**</u> <u>IT MATTERS NOT HOW THE BABYLONIAN JEWS HIDE THE TRUTH OF BLACK PEOPLE, THE TRUTH WILL RESURFACE.</u>

<u>**NO ONE CAN TAKE OUR TRUTH FROM US, THE BLACK RACE BECAUSE THE TRUTH IS ENGRAINED – ETCHED IN OUR DNA. AND IT MATTERS NOT HOW MAN TRY TO CHANGE IT, ALTER THE TRUTH OF LIFE (HISTORY) THEY CANNOT.**</u>

LISTEN MAN CAN CHANGE THE FLESH BUT THEY CANNOT CHANGE YOUR TRUE DNA WHICH IS THE SPIRIT. HENCE THE FLESH IS NOT LIFE THE SPIRIT IS.

The full truth must be told and it is telling right now.

Hence no matter how these Babylonian Liars tell lies against the Black Race and Good God and Allelujah, they will never prosper **BECAUSE TIME WILL TELL AND IT IS TELLING RIGHT NOW.**

Remember I told you above that I was asking Good God not to allow any Babylonian Jew into his kingdom. <u>**So it matters not what these White Liars do**</u>

because they are INFINITELY AND INDEFINITELY MORE THAN FOREVER EVER WITHOUT END LOCKED OUT OF GOOD GOD'S KINGDOM AND ABODE. THIS I GUARANTEE IN LIVING AND IN DEATH. You don't lie like that come on now.

Good God did not lock you out of his kingdom and abode; you locked yourselves out with the lies you tell and the killings that you do each and every day.

LIFE DOES NOT SACRIFICE, NOR DOES LIFE MAKE SACRIFICES, DEATH DOES. YOU HAVE TO SACRIFICE YOUR LIFE TO DEATH FOR A PLACE IN HELL AND THIS IS WHAT BILLIONS GLOBALLY HAS AND HAVE DONE. SO NONE OF US CAN BLAME GOOD GOD AND ALLELUJAH FOR OUR FAILURES AND MISGIVINGS, BUT I CAN AND HAVE DONE SO BECAUSE I'VE MADE HIM MY TRUTH AND ALL YOU DIDN'T.

*Yes I know not all **WHITE JEW FALL UNDER THE BABYLONIAN BANNER OF DEATH BECAUSE NOT ALL BLACKS ARE BLACKS. HENCE NOT ALL WHITES ARE WHITES.** (See the Ying and Yang and it matters not if you look at the white and blue Ying and Yang which is the Blue and White Nile).*

You cannot band with the Devil and or Satan and write books of lies about the God that you say is your Father. You follow BABYLONIAN LAW AND LAWS, HENCE YOU FALL UNDER THE BANNER OF BABYLON.

You write lies not truth and think in all that you do to change history it will work. It will not work. Like Eve (Evening) you listened to the devil, MARRIED THE DEVIL (interlocking six pointed star and or triangles) and think Good God and Allelujah will not walk away from you and your lies.

You the Babylonian Jews say, you are chosen. BUT LET ME TELL YOU THIS, YOU ARE NOT THE TRUE JEWS, HENCE YOU WILL NEVER EVER BE THE CHOSEN; THE TRUE CHOSEN JEWS. YOU NEVER WERE CHOSEN AND NEVER WILL BE CHOSEN.

YOU ARE NOT THE TRUE JEWS, HENCE NONE OF YOU WILL GO UP TO SEE GOOD GOD AND ALLELUJAH BECAUSE NOT ONE OF YOUR NAMES ARE WRITTEN IN THE BOOK OF LIFE. ***ABSOLUTELY NO BABYLONIAN NAME IS WRITTEN IN THE BOOK OF LIFE. EVERY TRUE JEW KNOWS THIS.***

But Ethiopia. **NOT EVEN ONE ETHIOPIAN NAME IS WRITTEN IS THE BOOK OF LIFE BECAUSE ETHIOPIA ORIGINALLY SOLD OUT GOOD GOD; HENCE THE HATRED FOR THEM BY GOOD GOD AND ALLELUJAH HIMSELF.** And like I said, Good God does not hate. I asked the question as to why God hated Ethiopians and was shown, not told, but shown why. So whether life started in Ethiopia it matters to me not BECAUSE *ETHIOPIA LOST THE ARK OF THE COVENANT LONG BEFORE ADAM AND EVE OF YOUR HOLY BOOK OF SIN AND DECEIT.* Your Free Mason and or Illuminati book – YES THE BOOK OF ETHERS FOR THOSE WHO KNOW.

AND YES THE FIRE BOOK AND OR THE BOOK OF RAM (QURAN) FOR THOSE WHO KNOW THE BOOK THIS WAY.

So yes, the true Jews know the truth and it matters not what the Babylonian Jews say. And like I said, not all

Jews – White Jews fall under the Babylonian Banner. You as Babylonian Jews knew your end was 2013 and or 1313 in spiritual time which is December 2013 in modern day and time. **YOU KNEW YOU WOULD BE LOCKED OUT OF GOOD GOD'S KINGDOM; SO YOU DECEIVED BILLIONS AND SENT THEM TO HELL WITH YOUR LIES; YOUR SO CALLED HOLY BIBLE.** *SO BECAUSE YOU DECEIVED THEM (BILLIONS) AND LIED TO THEM, ALL YOUR NAMES MUST BE TAKEN OUT OF THE BOOK OF LIFE FOR WHAT YOU HAVE DONE AND RIGHTFULLY SO. Thus saith the Lord thy God meaning it is so.*

You cannot lie to people like this because **_LIFE IS NOT ABOUT DEATH, IT'S ABOUT GOOD AND TRUE LIFE._**

EVERY HUMAN BEING INCLUDING THE DEVIL'S CHILDREN GOT THE OPPORTUNITY TO AMEND THEIR WICKED AND EVIL WAYS, BUT BECAUSE OF LIES, HUMANS CONTINUED WITH THE LIE; CONTINUED WITH THEIR EVIL WAYS. This was what the 24000 years was for. It was for death's and or evil's children to amend their ways and save self but this they could not do so. They continued with the lie thus deceiving billions and sending them straight to hell. *So because there was no amendment of ways;* **DEATH COMES ON A MASSIVE**

SCALE TO TAKE HIS OWN; ALL WHO BOW DOWN TO HIM AS WELL AS PRAISE HIM.

Yes the devil took some of Good God's children and or people with him and this is a crying shame because we did forget that he Good God would never ever give the devil control of his people. He would not give the devil and or anyone evil his power and we know this. Bob Marley also told you this in TIME WILL TELL when he said, **"JAH WILL NEVER GIVE THE POWER TO A BALD HEAD."**

Yes many of his Good God's children used their power to do evil but the penalty is on them. They are going to have to answer for their crimes, hence I truly do not forgive her for what she has done to me because she did wrong in the sight of Man and Good God come on now.

We choose to sin and die instead of telling the truth and live. I did wrong I have to own up to my wrongs. Why lie and add more time on my sentence of death. If I can clear up those sins with the good I do, I am going to do good come on now.

I know there is no water in hell. My spirit needs water to live, so why would I go to hell to face sufferings and pain; drought? I need water to survive, so how am I going to survive in hell? Here on earth my spirit is showing me when I disobey I will go to hell and feel worse pain than this, so why would I not listen to my spirit and live for truth?

So no it matters not the hatred I will receive from the White and or Babylonian Jews. **IF YOU CARRIED THE TRUTH, AND KNEW THE TRUTH, YOU WOULD NOT BE LIVING BY LIES AND TELLING LIES. NOR WOULD YOU BE CONDEMNING BILLIONS BECAUSE OF YOUR HATRED FOR AND OF THEM.** REMEMBER, REVELATIONS DID REVEAL. REVELATIONS DID SAY, **"WOE BE UNTO THE JEWS THAT CALL THEMSELVES JEWS BECAUSE THEY ARE OF THE SYNAGOGUE OF SATAN."** So truly good luck to all of you because it did say woe be unto you.

So truly woe be unto you BECAUSE:

NO ISRAELITE CAN BE JEWISH.

IF YOU ARE AN ISRAELITE YOU CANNOT BE JEWISH AND YOU WILL

NEVER EVER BE ACCEPTED AS JEWISH BECAUSE YOU ARE ISRAELITE. Thus saith the Lord thy God, meaning it is so. YOU DO NOT FALL UNDER THE JEWISH BANNER, SO TRULY GOOD LUCK TO YOU AND YOUR LIES. You fall under Babylonian Banner and every true Jew knows this. Ethiopia relinquished all rights to Good God long ago. Therefore Good God abandoned them just like he did Eve (Evening), so truly good luck to the lots of you. Therefore, Ethiopia lost the Ark of the Covenant. They do not have it because they do not fall under the protection of Good God and Allelujah, THE JEWISH BANNER. And yes this is why BLACK PEOPLE can be found in India and remnants of their (Black People's history) can be found in Pakistan until this day. And yes factor in Nimrod into the equation if you need and want to. Yep factor in Adam and Abraham too.

Now I ask you this, IF HE GOOD GOD HATES YOU, HOW THE HELL CAN YOU SAY YOU ARE HIS PEOPLE WHEN HE GOOD GOD AND ALLELUJAH KNOWS NOT YOU AND OR KNOWS YOU NOT?

NO LIAR CAN ENTER GOOD GOD'S ABODE, SO WHAT SAY YOU WHO HAVE WRITTEN LIES AND TOLD LIES ON HIM GOOD GOD AND ALLELUJAH TO KEEP YOUR PLACE AND MONEY WITH DEATH? Good God never told any of us to write books of lies about him or on him. Good God never told us to believe in lies or accept lies.

We as humans are the ones to defile him Good God and self, and because of this we have to pay. We have to pay the consequences because we were specifically told, <u>"THE WAGES OF SIN IS DEATH."</u> We are the ones to ignore this law and warning sign and die.

WE'VE FORGOTTEN THAT DEATH DOES NOT COME RIGHT AWAY WHEN WE SIN. DEATH TAKES TIME TO COME BECAUSE IF IT'S THE ONE THING DEATH HAS, IT'S TIME.

<u>**LIFE – GOOD AND TRUE LIFE HATH NOT TIME, BECAUSE GOOD AND TRUE LIFE IS EVERLASTING AND OR ETERNAL; CANNOT DIE.**</u>

We've forgotten that death does not have to take you for your sins. Death can take your child, your mother, father, sister, cousin, or uncle in lieu of you. **DEATH HAS NO**

MY TALK – BOOK FIVE

RULES TO PLAY BY WHEN IT COMES TO YOUR SINS AND OR GENERATIONAL SINS.

From your family sin and have not made amends for his or her sins, then death can take whomever in your family because your family belongs to him; you owe him and you are indebted to him.

What about female death?

From what I see and or gather now. Female death are for the messengers because as a chosen and or child or God; Good God and Allelujah you have certain gifts including the gift the stop death, and if you piss off death, she is the one to take you and take everything in sight. Yes including the land that messenger lives in.

She is fierce hence truly don't piss her off.

Can certain lands be saved?

Yes but that is not for me to determine. Like I said, my homeland of Jamaica can be saved but I do not trust the people to save self and land. Too much wickedness is upon the land already and the land was deemed unclean by Good God himself. Further, the writing in the sky did say JamaicaF but this land still has a chance. I know this *for a fact. But like I said I do not trust my own to save land and self.*

America I truly do not know about because I've seen their fall. I did see their destruction. But with all this said, there is something deep down inside of me that is holding on to them; hope and I truly do not know why. I dream about this land and people virtually every night; so in truth SOMEONE OR SOMETHING DO NOT WANT ME TO GIVE UP ON THEM.

There is something gnawing inside of me for them and I truly do not know what it is. I cannot find a common ground for them because this is a land that values death over life. <u>*This land houses the key to life; true life, but instead of preserving true life, they destroy it. Hence I cannot have any compassion for them.*</u> *No, I am not heartless but I have to be strong and not fall at the wayside because I know the wickedness of America the United States of America.*

YOU CANNOT HAVE LIFE AND TAKE FROM LIFE LIKE THIS.

YOU CANNOT HAVE LIFE AND DISRESPECT LIFE COME ON NOW. *It's like in the dream how she and the white man was* *disrespecting God – Good God. Their wrongs hurt me and the wrongs of America did hurt the black race of old and today. I have to think of the babies that died, cried out in pain because of the injustice of the demon seeds that resided on that land.*

GOOD GOD GAVE AMERICA, THE UNITED STATES OF AMERICA HIS LIFE IN THE SPIRITUAL REALM. THE UPRIGHT EYE IN TRIANGLE IS SPIRITUAL LIFE AND FROM YOU HAVE THIS LIFE, YOU ARE GUARANTEED A PLACE WITH GOOD GOD NO MATTER WHAT. <u>PEOPLE THIS IS THE LIFE SATAN WANTED. SATAN WANTED SPIRITUAL LIFE AND AMERICA; THE UNITED STATES OF AMERICA HAD THIS AND DESTROYED IT FOR WHAT.</u> SO NO, I CANNOT HAVE COMPASSION FOR THEM JUST LIKE I CANNOT HAVE IT ANYMORE FOR MY JAMAICAN OWN. BOTH LANDS

(ISRAEL AND JUDAH) DESTROYED THE LIFE HE GOOD GOD AND ALLELUJAH HAS AND HAVE GIVEN THEM. HENCE LIFE MUST GO BACK TO THE EAST FOR PRESERVATION. <u>THUS GOOD GOD CAME TO HIS OWN AND THEY REFUSED HIM YET AGAIN.</u>

Hence **AFRICANS ARE GOING TO PAY AND PAY DEARLY BECAUSE THEY DID ALLOW THE DEVIL AND HIS DEMON SEEDS TO MASSACRE AND KILL THEIR BELOVED OWN.**

I have no compassion for evil, hence I will repeat, <u>if I am the saving grace for humanity, I will infinitely and indefinitely never ever forever ever never ever save anyone that is wicked and evil because they know what they were doing.</u> They willingly and knowingly participate in evil; wrongs, so why should I or anyone save them or even die to save them? You are evil, so why the hell should I have compassion for you?

Like I've said, if the lie did not work for Eve, (Evening), how is the lie and the Jesus lie going to work for you?

Life isn't a game but yet we treat it as a game anyway. The mass extinction of man is coming, but yet we are not taking life seriously and this is bullshit on our part. Your life is coming to a brutal end, wake up.

It's amazing how Good God has tried over the ages to show us that evil and or sin is not our friend, but yet we keep refusing the truth; Him. Like I said, **I truly don't care if the White Jews or anyone hates me. This is your bleeping life, do all to make amends for your sins.** YES I KNOW CERTAIN SINS ARE NOT FORGIVEN, BUT IT DOES NOT MEAN YOU ARE NOT TO TRY TO MAKE AMENDS FOR THEM. KEEP TRYING BECAUSE EVERYONE HAS A SAVING GRACE DESPITE WHAT I WRITE. **YOU ARE YOUR SAVING GRACE NOT ME BECAUSE I WAS NOT SENT FOR BILLIONS, I WAS SENT FOR THE TRUE AND RIGHTEOUS; GOOD GOD'S OWN.**

YOU KNOW TRUTH IS EVERLASTING LIFE. **YOU CANNOT BE DENIED ACCESS TO LIFE IF YOU LIVE TRUTHFULLY.**

NO, GOOD GOD CANNOT DENY YOU ACCESS SO TRULY DON'T GO THERE WITH IT.

TRUTH IS EVERLASTING AND OR ETERNAL LIFE; SO TRULY DON'T GO THERE.

But you said you were praying and asking God; Good God not to let Babylonian Jews in?

YES BUT THE FINAL DECISION TO LET YOU IN IS NOT MINE, **IT IS UP TO YOU AND GOOD GOD AND ALLELUJAH.** HE KNOWS THE FUTURE BETTER THAN I. AND I CAN PRAY TO HIM FOR THIS, BUT IT DOES NOT MEAN HE LISTENS TO ME. HE IS THE FINAL DECISION MAKER NOT ME, HENCE I WILL TELL YOU TO NEVER GIVE UP ON GOODNESS; YOUR TRUTH AND GOOD ROAD.

Know that things do change in the spiritual realm. THE ONLY THING THAT DOES NOT CHANGE AND WILL NEVER CHANGE IS DEATH. DEATH CANNOT CHANGE AND WE ALL KNOW THIS. So stop living for death and start living your life good and true. You know the flesh is a trap for the spirit,

so free yourself from the sins in your life and the sins that surround you.

Yes I know the hell wicked and evil people must face. THEY ARE GUARANTEED A PLACE IN HELL AND THIS CANNOT CHANGE WITH THEM. THEY DID ALL FOR EVIL, <u>BUT IT DOES NOT MEAN A TRUTHFUL PERSON CANNOT HAVE COMPASSION FOR THEM AND PETITION GOOD GOD FOR THEM,</u> BUT I REFUSE TO. I REFUSE TO SAVE THEM BECAUSE OF THE EVILS THEY HAVE DONE.

I refuse to petition Good God for wicked and evil people but it does not mean someone else cannot. They can as long as they are ordained to do so.

Will there be another after you?

<u>I truly do not know and I truly hope not because humans have had chance after chance to save self and wasted it.</u> Instead of choosing life; humans choose death. So billions have to live with the decision they've made. This may seem contradictory, but I am hoping it is not. <u>**Good God has and have tried time and time again and WE AS HUMANS ARE THE ONES TO FAIL HIM, SO I TRULY HOPE THERE IS NO MORE AFTER ME.**</u> ***<u>EVIL MUST STOP AND IF I CAN END IT NOW, THEN I</u>***

AM GOING TO DO SO WITH EVERY FABRIC OF TRUTH AND TRUE LOVE WITHIN ME FOR MY TRUE OWN, WHICH IS GOOD GOD'S TRUE OWN. AND YES, I REFUSE TO PETITION GOOD GOD AND ALLELUJAH TO SEND ANOTHER AFTER ME TO SAVE HUMANITY BECAUSE IN TRUTH, WE ARE NOT DESERVING OF IT GIVEN THE WICKEDNESS AND EVILS THAT WE DO HERE ON EARTH AND IN THE SPIRITUAL REALM.

EVIL HAS AND HAVE DONE ENOUGH DAMAGE TO OUR LIVES, EARTH, WATERWAYS; ENVIRONMENT AND IT HAS TO STOP. EARTH, YOU, ME, THE ENVIRONMENT, THE UNIVERSE AND GOOD GOD AND ALLELUJAH DO NOT DESERVE IT. Every chance we get we disrespect Good God and Allelujah. So why the hell would I petition Him to send someone else after me to save wicked and evil people? Ungrateful people that would rather kill life than cherish and preserve life. Life isn't only human, the air we breathe is life also, but we pollute it, take away from life.

The water that we drink is life, but yet we pollute it, take away from life. So no, I will not petition Good God and

Allelujah to send anymore messengers to save you and or anyone after my spirit leaves my flesh. I refuse to. YOU DO NOT LIVE TO KILL AND OR LIVE TO DIE AND EXPECT GOOD GOD TO SAVE YOU. YOUR CHOICE IS DEATH, SO GOOD AND TRUE LIFE MUST BE TAKEN FROM YOU AND THIS IS WHAT HE GOOD GOD AND ALLELUJAH IS DOING AND RIGHTFULLY SO.

YOUR DEATH COMES NOW AND RIGHTFULLY SO BECAUSE NOT ONE OF YOU IN THE LIVING THOUGHT ABOUT LIFE AND THE IMPACT YOUR SINS WOULD HAVE ON LIFE.

YOU SAY YOU WANT LIFE BUT YET YOU KILL LIFE. SO YOU TRULY DON'T WANT LIFE THEN, HENCE TRUTH, GOOD GOD AND ALLELUJAH MUST SAVE HIS OWN AND LEAVE DEATH'S CHILDREN TO DEATH; ALONE.

HE'S TAKEN US OUT OF OUR MESSES AND WE GO RIGHT BACK INTO THE MESSES HE'S TAKEN US OUT OF.

HE FREED US FROM SLAVERY, BUT YET WE CONTINUE WITH OUR SLAVE MENTALITY.

WE'VE BECOME SO HEARTLESS AND COLD THAT WE CARE NOT FOR EACH OTHER. WE HATE BASED ON RELIGION, RACE, SEXUAL PREFERENCE AND ORIENTATION.

WE'VE BECOME SO HATEFUL THAT WE HATE BASED ON SKIN TONE; SKIN COLOUR; HUE.

AS HUMANS WE KNOW HOW VILE WE'VE BECOME, BUT YET REFUSE TO STOP THE NONSENSE OF HATRED. SO BECAUSE OF THIS WE MUST BE DESTROYED BECAUSE WE'VE BECOME THE CHILDREN OF SODOM AND GOMORRAH. WE ARE THEM HENCE THE BULLSHIT THAT SOME HUMANS DO UNTIL THIS DAY.

WE ARE THE ONES TO SIN AND DESTROY SELF BECAUSE WE LISTENED TO THE BABYLONIANS THAT TELL US OTHERWISE. GOOD GOD GAVE US GOOD AND TRUE LIFE, WHY WOULD HE TAKE IT FROM US?

Go back to your so called holy bible and read for yourself from Genesis to revelations the lies that have been told to you. Yesterday was April 22, 2015 and my eldest son and I were talking just to interrupt the flow of this book, and he said, Adam and Eve were the first creations and I told him no; they were not. Go back and read Genesis again, the first creation Good God blessed, but when it came to Adam, Good God did not bless him. He talked about Cain and Abel and I told him, ***if Adam and Eve were the first creation, why would Cain make reference to him being killed if he went into another land?***

So now I ask you, if Adam and Eve were the first creation, how did Cain know about them (these people) and where did they come from? So if Cain knew about them, then Adam and Eve must have known about them. **So vile and wicked human beings were on the land long before Adam and Eve come on now.**

He (my son) talked about Abraham and how Abraham fed the Lord. I told him Abraham never fed the Lord and or God. What the bible was referencing were the angels. **AND TO SET THE RECORD STRAIGHT, ANGELS DO NOT EAT HUMAN FOOD. HENCE MAN NOT ONLY TELL LIES ON GOOD GOD, THEY TELL LIES ON HIS MESSENGERS; ANGELS ALSO.**

Like I've said, time and time again, life is given, we are the ones to live it good and clean. As humans Good God cannot constantly be trying to save us and we keep choosing death as our stay. THERE IS A BIG DIFFERENCE BETWEEN LIFE AND DEATH. Death hath no life and we all know this but yet we choose to die anyway. Look at a dead body. Does that body have life?

No right?

So then why do you think you have life when you choose death? This is what you will become when you choose death. Like unto a dead body. So if you don't know, now you know. You have the truth because the truth cannot lie, nor can the truth deceive and you all know this but you choose the latter anyway.

Yes you will doubt God; Good God and your journey, I do. I was in LA and I keep dreaming about LA but yet I am in doubt because I see destruction and now the Rock, Dwayne Johnson has a movie coming out depicting the destruction and or devastation of LA; so now I am doubting my visions by saying this movie was what I was picking up on.

I am questioning myself and my visions as of late when it comes to the United States of America. As messengers and children of God; Good God we doubt him at times. This is normal because things are not falling into place like they should. Right now they are not falling into place for me as they should and this is sad. Yes my heart is weak when it comes to compassion for this land like I've said above, but I cannot be weak because the damage was done. Condemnation is upon this land and this has nothing to do with me. **_The shot has been fired more than once and I have to step aside and let death do his and her job. I could not save this destruction of land because I was too late. This is ordained, hence it's a spiritual doing that must manifest on land real soon._**

Also, if I had compassion for the United States, I would have to have it for my homeland Jamaica. I would also have to have it for Germany, Luxembourg, all Babylonian lands and I cannot do this. I cannot be weak when it comes to America.

Yes I am in a state of confusion and I cannot let this confusion get the best of me. All I know is Good God's children and people must flee out of Babylon right now lest they be consumed. I truly do not know the extent of the damage and or destruction. All I know is life is going to be lost and like I said, I cannot have compassion for America, the United States of America. **_Marcus Mosiah Garvey warned them and they crucified him by slandering him and I am no different._** Yes I know the upright eye in triangle, but this land forfeited this right when they rejected and slaughter (slandered) him, Marcus Mosiah Garvey. Like I said in some of my other books**, LIFE CAME TO LIFE AND LIFE REJECTED LIFE.** So because of this I was not permitted to save them. The destruction of America, the United States of America has been ordained and it's their own doing, because they design weapons of mass destruction and diseases to kill and they did kill. **_Thus the national debt they've amassed they cannot repay, nor can they repay the debt of the lives they've taken over the centuries._** Hence the iniquity of the Amorites is not yet full.

I am missing the point and my flight when it comes to America and I can no longer do this. I have to stay focused and not let cold and heartless people get the best of me.

Dreamt I was in a subway going somewhere. Where I cannot tell you because the escalators were long and going in different directions and some went up in the air. One particular one I wanted to go on went up, and when I came to the edge of the landing I had to jump down to get on this escalator and the jump would have hurt me; hence I moved away from this area and took another route. The route I took I forgot my purse with all my documents in it. I thought if I went back I would not find my purse because someone would have taken it, so I let things be. I went on ahead in confusion because I could not get to my destination. I was taking the wrong track and or escalator. And for you who are wondering, these escalators were made out of black belt – conveyor belts but never the less they were escalators.

Dreamt I was at the airport and I was talking to this lady; young white lady but I cannot tell you what she looks like. All I know is she boarded her flight and I missed mine. When I was ready to board my flight I was two hours late, my flight left. Looking at the clock I saw 9:15 so I am missing something in my life and I truly do not know what it is.

I can't keep talking and missing what I am truly suppose to do. Like I said, there is confusion in my life right now and I truly do not know how to correct this confusion.

I also dreamt I was with this White Guy, we walked into this grocery store together. He was not in black but brown which is good for me. I truly loathe black and red on people in the spirit realm and in my dreams and or visions.

At the entrance of the store was pork and cheese; cheese that smelt bad. We held on to each other and passed the stench that was to the left side of us. So that part of our life we overcame because we both smelt the stench. Hence obeah and or the devil has not stopped and will not stop working in my life. I just had to say that because I know the problems and pressures in my friend's life. And he's not one to tell you of his troubles, nor is he one to ask for help and this is sad. Proud to the end I would say, so I just have to let him be because a lot of my confusion surrounds him. I guess in life people aren't forthcoming when it comes to life. You ask for something but yet can't handle it; don't know how to handle a truthful and caring person. Hence I quarrel with God – Good God as well. Why ask for something and or someone and when they are totally truthful and honest with you, you cannot handle it and or you push that person away.

NOT EVERYONE IN LIFE LIVE TO HURT AND DECEIVE.
NOT EVERYONE IN LIFE IS A GOLD DIGGER. *And yes from what I see now, I am infinitely not sure of humans now a days because many live to lie, cheat and deceive.* ***Hence I truly do not want or need to be amongst people in society. My upbringing is different, and I am truly glad that I was raised right not just in the***

sight of man but in the sight of Good God and Allelujah and he Good God and Allelujah cannot say otherwise. I refuse to live like the wicked and evil of society.

I REFUSE TO BE STINGY IN ANYTHING.

I LOATE MISERLY AND STINGY PEOPLE; HENCE I TRULY DO NOT WANT AND NEED THEM AROUND ME. LIFE IS NOT STINGY, SO NO ONE SHOULD BE STINGY IN ANYTHING WHETHER THAT ANYTHING BE AFFECTION AND TRUTH; TRUE LOVE. And besides true love cannot be stingy in any way.

To continue on with the dream; after we passed the pork with fermented and or stinky cheese, we went from isle to isle. We did not walk together meaning we were not holding hands. I somehow went to this section that had batteries and I picked up Duracell Batteries the C batteries. I had to interfere with the package and took one out that I could not put back in, but one of the attendant in the grocery store was nice enough to put the battery back in for me. I asked him, the White Guy that I was with who was a bit taller than me and had a pudgy (tummy) if we were forever ever; a life time? I think at first he did not answer so I asked him again, and he said yes. But people with all that said, I felt him to be cold, I did not feel any warmth in him. **Hence I have to**

ask what does it profit a man woman or child to be cold and heartless; void of truth and true love?

Touch and feel is so important to me that I cherish it.

We feel warmth people; so at what point in our lives and or what could possibly hurt us so bad for us to become so cold and heartless?

I've been through hell and the book Behind the Scars written by me tells you a little insist as to what I've been through in life. This book I cannot edit nor can I look upon because some of my pain is written here; in this book. I cannot finish this book nor will I finish it because that part of my life is over. <u>I have to do all to heal myself and move on.</u> I was told I was the target of death, I am the one that death wanted to kill and I truly do not know why?

Why am I the target for death?
Why does death have to come after me?
Why isn't Good God truly trying to protect me by not allowing death to come my way?

Life is beautiful but what's the point of having a beautiful life when death targets you all the time?

So yes I am a crossroad. And yes I know what this dream means with the White man; hence I am dreaming that I am missing my flight because something is truly not right with him. Yes I want to help but all I can do is encourage and lend strength this way.

<u>If someone is blocking you out of there life you have to let it be because the pork and stinky cheese is truly not a good start to a lasting friendship or union.</u> I have to live by my truth and like I've said, I truly do not want or need cold and heartless people around me.

Life is truly not about pain for pain. No one has to go through pain alone. IF SOMETHING IS HURTING YOU AND YOU TRUST THAT PERSON THAT IS SAYING LET ME HELP YOU, THEN LET THE PERSON HELP YOU. I KNOW PEOPLE ARE NOT LIKE ME AND IT'S HARD TO TRUST; THEN TRULY RELY ON GOOD GOD AND ALLELUJAH TO GET YOU THROUGH. LET HIM HELP YOU THEN. LET HIM GOOD GOD AND ALLELUJAH BE ALL THAT YOU NEED. No one has to live in pain come on now. Do all that you can to help you because despite the writings in these books, there's still good people out there. I need to do good for you, so allow me to do the good that I can do for you so that you can help yourself come on now. Good God and Allelujah is this way. So let him do all the

good that he can for you because he truly loves you and not just loves you so. I know this. I know he truly loves me but I am down on him because I want and need evil to be gone right away. Evil lost in 2013, so I am expecting evil to go now and not stay. I need good to be separated from evil hence the final separation of lands must take place and it is going to happen, <u>*but I need Good God and Allelujah's people to be safe and secure so that when death comes to take their own, Good God and Allelujah's children and people which is you are safe and secure with him.*</u>

<u>**So yes I know what this dream means.**</u> I know that he is not ordained for me because my emotions are flying for him but he is not clean; spiritually clean for me. **<u>Good God has not ordained him for me.</u>** So I am being warned despite my comfort level with him. The road with him to cleanliness and good food is not the right road for me. **THE START IS DIRTY; HENCE MY LIFE AND END; <u>OUR LIFE AND END WILL BE DIRTY.</u>** Any yes I am hoping I've explained it right for you to comprehend. <u>**The start is dirty hence nothing that we do will be clean.**</u> So I have to adhere to the right and righteous road that I am travelling on. I cannot miss my mark with Good God; hence I cannot let a shirt or a skirt take me off the path that I am on. I have to stay clean despite my emotions and feel of him.

Sad yes but this is my reality with men. To so far they are truly not clean. Well the ones I've chosen for me anyway.
SO IN ALL THAT WE DO, IF YOU ARE CHOSEN BY GOOD GOD HE DOES DO ALL TO WARN YOU SO THAT YOU STAY ON THE RIGHT PATH.

Listen I live a boring life and I wanted to go have a drink, my spirit was latching onto drinking. Suffice it to say, I did not have a drink, I had coffee and a blueberry muffin with a friend. Someone that my spirit forbids me to be with, but I wanted to be disobedient because stress took me reckless and rude with finding out that the apartment I live in, is going to start charging hydro and the rate being fished around was between $200-$300.00 every 60 days and I cannot afford this. Man stress took me because I know I will be in the streets with my children. I am looking for a place and a junior 1 bedroom is over 900.00$ plus and you have to pay parking and hydro. So by the time I am finished paying my rent and bills, I cannot afford to buy anything, nor can I afford to buy any medical supplies not covered by the government. So yes stress took over to the point where I wanted a drink to numb my senses and go to sleep.

Like I said, I did not have any alcohol and I am thankful I did not get any and did not do anything nasty with this person though he wanted to. I truly don't know what it is with some Black Men. You are a friend and all you want to do is talk and they want something else. They know you are trying to keep yourself clean but yet they want you to dirty yourself with them. Yes I am to blame for this because I know my spirit truly does not like him for me in that way. He's forbidden to me and due to disobedience I walked the folly ground. So if anything had happened, I could not blame him, I would have to blame myself because my spirit forbids me to be with him because he's not right; clean and I know this. I would be punished severely, so I truly have to watch myself and my stress load.

I truly do not have female friend's family. I truly do not have one apart from my sister and my niece. Male friends I have 5, but it's getting where friendship is not on the mind of two. Relationship is and I truly don't want that because I am not interested in that way and I've stated this, but the message is so not getting across. **_Friendship is friendship to me when it comes to certain people._** **_I see life with you before anything escalates, hence the friends with benefits crap does not work with me._** I truly don't need it. My body is so not attracted to you in that way; hence you are wasting your time. I know who I want and need to lay with hence I leave things alone. I am there for you as a friend, so accept that and not want to take it further.

Off track again. Hence my dream with me being in the grocery store and with this White Guy I know what it means. I've come to a crossroad in my life and that crossroad is confusing and it is an heartache. I am missing my flight and what I need to do and I cannot continue to let this happen. I have a job to do and I have to do it. **_Thus I am learning more and more that a person without truth cannot truly love; hath not a clean heart and or soul._**

Is this disheartening?

It is in many ways. **_I also have to remember; you cannot give your truth to people that are not capable of truth; true love. You are giving your truth in vain._**

I cannot change a person, that person have to want better for self and change self for the better. Yes it's easy to love, but when that love hath no truth then what is the point?

You cannot give of you to someone that does not want you.

You cannot want better for someone that does not want you to want or need better for them.

You cannot feel for feelingless people; cold and heartless people because they are incapable of true truth. This I am learning, hence I truly hope Good God learns this too. So yes, I feel what he Good God feels when it comes to humans. He's been trying and we keep rejecting him. We keep telling him **NO** with our actions.

So what is the point of him giving his truth and true love to people that truly do not want it?

What is the point of giving his truth and true love to people who waste it (his truth and true love)?

What is the point of providing for people that truly don't want or need Him?

Is it hard to learn this?

Yes because I still cannot figure out at what point in time a man and or humans got to the point of coldness and heartlessness? And I am sorry if I confused you with my wording because I too am confused. Could not find the right words to put this sentence in. **<u>Hence a person that hath not truth cannot truly love.</u>**

Knowing these things and seeing these things, do I want to change?

I would like to but I can't. I cannot change my caring nature towards truth and true love. This nature is engrained in me. **<u>Hence I have to be careful who I give my care and truth to.</u>** It's not everyone that is deserving of truth because it's not everyone that knows truth and can do and live by the truth, and this is truly a shame and a pity. So as there is no warmth in man; truth on earth, there is not warmth in spirits in the spiritual realm and this is a total shame. **<u>Hence true love is rarer than I truly know. Just as the dead in flesh hath no feelings, so is the dead in spirit in the spiritual realm; they have no feelings.</u>**

A man woman or child that is cold on earth cannot be warm in the spiritual realm.

SO WITHOUT TRUTH AND TRUE LOVE, A MAN WOMAN OR CHILD INCLUDING BEAST CANNOT LIVE BECAUSE THEY KNOW NOT THE VALUE OF GOOD AND TRUE LIFE.

They have not care because care resides not in them. So in all I've been shown, I have my warning signs and I am heeding my call. I know the truth of how Good God feels when it comes to man; humanity.

<u>We say we love but have not truth because we continue sinning in the flesh; hence we die in the spirit; hell.</u>

So for you Israelis that are going to come at me and say I am a damned liar you are Jewish, prove to me and Good God Himself your Jewishness. <u>*You can't even praise right but yet you say you are of Good God and Allelujah.*</u>

Prove to Good God and Allelujah and the world your Jewishness. You don't steal a man's history and or lineage and life story and say it is yours. <u>**IF YOU WERE THE TRUE JEWS YOU WOULD HAVE KNOWN THE TRUTH OF THE UNIVERSE AND THE TRUTH OF THE ETHIOPIANS OF DAYS PAST; LONG AGO.** **Come on now.**</u>

You claim to be but are not, never will be. **JEWS ARE FORBIDDEN TO WALK IN THE WAYS OF THE WICKED AND EVIL BECAUSE THEY (THE WICKED AND EVIL; SINFUL) ARE NOT CLEAN. JEWS ARE CLEAN HENCE THEY FALL UNDER THE ORDER OF LIFE; GOOD GOD AND ALLELUJAH AND NOT UNDER THE ORDER OF DEATH.**

WE ARE NOT TO COMMUNE WITH THEM; THE WICKED AND EVIL; SINFUL AND SCORFUL. Psalms One

WE ARE NOT TO LIVE AMONGST THEM OR WITH THEM; THE WICKED AND EVIL OF SOCIETY; WORLD.

WE ARE NOT TO BEFRIEND THEM; THE WICKED AND EVIL. WE ARE TO LEAVE THEM ALONE BECAUSE THEIR VALUES AND GOD, IS NOT OUR VALUES AND GOD.

WE ARE OF LIFE AND THEY ARE OF THE DEAD; DEATH COME ON NOW.

YOU SHOULD KNOW THIS, BUT THEN AGAIN YOU'RE NOT THE REAL AND TRUE JEWS. HENCE YOU LIVE WRONG, PRAY WRONG, EAT, DRINK AND BREATHE WRONG; HENCE YOU ARE ALL WRONG ALL AROUND.

From you accept Ethiopia you accept Babylon; hence you joined forces with death against life; Good God and Allelujah. No one that is of life can raise the six pointed flag because the six pointed flag is death's flag. This also goes for the six pointed star of David. **_When you join the upright and or upward triangle and downward triangle YOU ARE JOINING DEATH._** THESE TRIANGLES SHOULD NEVER BE JOINED UNDER ANY CIRCUMSTANCES AND A

TRUE JEW THAT KNOWS HIS OR HER LINEAGE; LIFE WOULD KNOW THIS, BECAUSE THIS TRUTH IS ENGRAINED IN THEM. And if they forget, they will be reminded of this at some point in their life.

Hence Israel cannot be Judah because THE TWO LANDS AND NATION ARE INFINITELY NOT THE SAME. JUDAH FALLS UNDER THE BANNER OF LIFE AND ISRAEL FALL UNDER THE BANNER OF DEATH. Your flag shows it, so not one of you can say a thing.

There are no boobut buts. You lied and for this you must pay. Thus saith the Lord thy God meaning it is so. THE WHITE AND BLUE NILE NEVER RAN THROUGH ISRAEL.

YOUR BABYLONIAN COUNTERPARTS (EGYPTIANS) DIVERTED THE BLUE AND WHITE NILE BY DAMMING IT UP SO THAT IT COULD REACH YOU. Modern day Israel is not the land of Good God and Allelujah and will never be. So no one in Israel can claim Jewish lineage, you can only claim Babylonian lineage because this is the

lineage you accept and fall under. Hence ABRAHAM THE BABYLONIAN IS YOUR FATHER. You accepted Abraham hence you accepted Babylon. So because of this, you CANNOT FIGHT AGAINST PALESTINE BECAUSE THEY ARE YOUR BRETHRENS; BROTHERS AND SISTERS.

Listen it matters not what you say about me.

It matters not what you do to me. A damn liar will always be a damned liar and thief. YOU CANNOT STEAL THE BLACKMAN HISTORY AND LINEAGE AND SAY IT IS YOURS BECAUSE GOOD GOD AND ALLELUJAH IS NOT WHITE HE IS BLACK; FALL UNDER THE BLACK BANNER NOT WHITE BANNER. And this has nothing to do with hue; colour of skin. Every true Jew know this.

What about Palestine. None can claim Jewish lineage. The can claim Abraham because Abraham was Babylonian like them. Abraham did follow and or worship idols. He did practice human and animal sacrifices, hence Abraham was not of Black Lineage, he was of Babylonian and or Hindu descent. Yes he had dark skin and your Book of Sin told us this. **So if you follow Abraham or Abram, then you follow Satan; Sin because NO BABYLONIAN HAVE A PLACE WITH GOOD GOD. ABSOLUTELY NONE.** *Hence Revelations said in part, "Woe be unto the Jews that call themselves Jews because they are of the synagogue of Satan."*

This is how I know it and this is how I am relating it back to you. And like I said, I am not the final decision maker of who gets into Good God's kingdom and abode, **you and him are.** And I will repeat, if I am the saving grace for humanity and or of humanity, I will not save anyone that is wicked and evil. I refuse to and Good God cannot make me save them.

Like I said, I truly do not care if you say I am a fraud. I've done my job; the job He Good God and Allelujah required of me, and I've done it with truth and true love to the best of my ability. I refuse to cheat and deceive anyone because I truly do not like it for myself nor do I like it for Good God and Allelujah. Life is more than truly precious to me, so why the hell would I want to take yours?

Keep your life because you need it in the afterlife.

Well Jesus died for me; he shed his blood for me. And your point? **I refuse to take you from your Jesus and or your god.** Good God's children have nothing to do with Jesus. Jesus is death, he died. No one can die to save me or you; they have to live to save you. The goodness you do in the living can save your family in the grave. Meaning if you have more good than sins on your sin record and you are right with Good God and Allelujah, you can request some of your goodness to go to a family member. So yes, your family may have generational sins and you can help them in the living. But some are burning in hell right now. Yes but not all. There are certain sins that automatically takes you to hell right away. **Suicide is one of those sins.** If you commit suicide in the living you automatically go to hell, this I know for a fact. There is no escaping hell for you.

As messengers can we petition for this to change?

Yes, and if I've said no before, do forgive me. But this debt and or sin you can petition for. Like I've said, there are times when I want to go there due to hurt and pain, what I have to go through. When you are set a certain way, trust me you want to kill yourself; **HENCE I CANNOT FORGIVE HER FOR WHAT SHE DID TO ME. SHE BROKE ME PHYSICALLY AND SPIRITUALLY.** WHEN YOU ARE SPIRITUALLY BOUND, YOU WANT TO DIE. YOU WANT TO

COMMIT SUICIDE BECAUSE YOUR TIE IS NOT A PHYSICAL TIE PER SAY BUT A SPIRITUAL ONE. WHEN YOU ARE BOUND OR TIED SPIRITUALLY, NO ONE ON EARTH CAN BREAK THIS TIE, YOU HAVE TO GO THROUGH THE HELL THAT COMES ALONG WITH THIS.

YES YOU ARE BOUND FOR A TIME AND THEN YOU ARE RELEASED. HENCE MANY MESSENGERS DO NOT MAKE IT, SOME GO INSANE AND YES MANY HAVE DIED.

So if you've given yourself over to death truly good luck because once you are bound, you will not be released. That bound is for the rest of your spiritual life. You have to face hell before you die; so truly good luck to billions of you literally.

KNOW THAT WHEN YOU ARE CLEAN AND YOU START OFF WITH A DIRTY AND OR UNCLEAN PERSON, YOU CANNOT BECOME CLEAN. YOU WILL BE FOREVER DIRTY WITH THAT PERSON.

What if you leave the person?

Then yes, you can become clean because you are making yourself whole again.

***You are renewing your spirit and making yourself clean.* THEREFORE, IT IS WISE TO START OFF WITH CLEAN PEOPLE AND OR A CLEAN PERSON AND CONTINUE TO LIVE CLEAN; WHOLE.**

Does it mean that unclean person cannot become clean?

In many cases that unclean person cannot become clean. Remember evil cannot change, evil will always be evil, and unclean will always be unclean. This may seem contradictory but this is the best way I know of to explain what I am trying to say to you. Meaning if you are clean you cannot lay with unclean, you will become unclean like that person. So stay clean at all times so that your life can lift up; rise up to Good God and Allelujah.

What if that person wants and need to become clean?

Then he or she must come clean and live clean. **<u>They have to do it without you.</u>** Remember, unclean people are not receptive to clean people; hence it's wise to commune with clean people. Unclean and or evil people will always try to take you off your path to Good God and I've shown you this above. Some people are so selfish that the only person and or thing that they can see is self. Hence many are vain and live for self gratification. And the guy that has had so many surgeries come to mind. He seeks perfection but yet fail to see just how ugly and hideous he looks in the sight of Man and

God; Good God. **<u>Beauty radiates from within and if you are good, people will see this beauty.</u>** They will see the beauty in you and in the good that you do not just for self but for others.

Yes Angie lef di man an mek him walk clean.

You cannot change him; he must want and need change for self.

No, you cannot tie him. The crap you are going through you did not have to go through it. **<u>The man did not belong to you in the first place because he was not ordained by Good God for you.</u>** He Good God tried to show you your life with him, but you could not comprehend what he was trying to tell you. Just like he's showing me this guy and how he is. I have to walk away for the betterment of me and my life. And yes the betterment of Good God's life also. If he wants us to unite in a good and true way, **<u>he has to change him for the better and not for the worse, and truly good luck with this because not all want to change self for the better come on now.</u>**

Yes there is pain in our lives but we can heal. **BROKEN BUT I AM HEALED Byron Cage.** Listen, Good God is there to help you if you put your trust in him. It will not be easy to do this because we do falter, I do. I know the truth of Good God and Allelujah and yes I've told him time and time again that I want to leave him, but **_I refuse to leave him and go to another god._**

I refuse to commit adultery when I leave him because we are still married. I still have his wedding band. Me leaving him is like a vacation to get my thoughts together and not be so confused. I know if I leave him ***I WILL DIE BECAUSE I WOULD HAVE OPENED UP MY LIFE FOR DEATH AND HIS PEOPLE; HIS DEMONS TO SERIOUSLY HURT ME AND YES TAKE MY LIFE BRUTALLY. HENCE BLACK PEOPLE HAVE FACED SLAVERY FROM THEN UNTIL NOW AND CAN'T LEARN THAT WHEN WE LEAVE GOOD GOD AND ALLELUJAH WE ARE PUNISHED BRUTALLY AND WE ARE KILLED. THE DEVIL OWNS US THEN. AND DON'T YOU DARE TELL ME ABOUT JESUS BECAUSE IF YOU KNEW YOUR TRUE HISTORY AND LINEAGE, YOU WOULD KNOW THAT JESUS DID NOT EXIST.*** And you know what; I am not here to convince you otherwise. If you believe in Jesus, continue to believe in him. Jesus is not my keep,

Good God is and He is whom I more than truly and unconditionally truly love with all my truth and honesty. He Good God is good and true life, hence I choose him and walk with him in all that I do. He is my ups and downs, my true peace and joy including my UNHAPPINESS.

So if your god is Allah, Jesus, Buddha, Krishna, Jehovah, Selassie, Shiva or what have you then koodles to you, stay with them because my GOD IS NOT YOUR GOD.

Like I said, mine is truth and He does not sacrifice anyone to death. ***He does try but we are the ungrateful ones to deceive him. So it matters not what you think of me as long as my Lovey and True Love truly loves me.*** As long as I know he cares and protects me and will provide all my needs, stress wise, health wise, financial wise, spiritual wise, physically wise, food and water wise, environmentally wise, tree wise, air wise, clothes wise, shelter wise, foot wise (walking), transportation wise, and so much more, I am good to go. So Angie leave the man alone because he's told you time and time again he does not want you. You are the one to hitch up aundaneat di man peepee cluck cluck like yu a fowl. Git up and walk, go your ways, Allelujah, glory to God. Move, im nuh want yu, move, Good God a tell you. Look how long Gad; Good Gad a show yu di truth an yu sidung inna abuse. Yu nuh truly love yuself. **HAVE SOME DAMN SELF WORTH AND PRIDE AND LEF DI MAN.** Coo pan how imma pit (spit) pan yu an yu tek it.

Yu batta bruise an yu a tek eee.

A man that has no respect of self and his mother can never have respect for you or anyone.

Eee ha nothing to du wid upbringing sometimes. Somea wi as parents try, but if di pickney sey dem naah listen wey yu a go du? **Yes you can pray but Good God cannot change wickedness for the better.** You as a parent have to leave these kids alone to time (when they come of age) like I am doing to mine. And truly don't go there because death and or Sin asked for time and got time when it came to humans. Death and or Sin did not change his or her dirty ways; they continued to take lives by letting you sin rude and reckless. I told you in another book my children asked for time when it came to giving up my apartment and I did give them time. *But what did they do right after I gave them time?* Some went back to their dirty and unlawful ways. The stress is off them but trust me they don't know what a clock a strike. **This is the same with Good God. HE'S GIVEN US 24000 YEARS TO AMEND OUR DIRTY WAYS AND INSTEAD OF CLEANING UP SELF, WE CONTINUE ON WITH OUR DIRTY WAYS. WE DID NOT CLEAN UP SELF; HENCE THE**

DESTRUCTION OF MAN COMES BEFORE 2032. WE ARE THE ONES TO PROVE TO GOOD GOD AND DEATH THAT HUMANS CANNOT BE TRUSTED.

WE ARE LIARS AND DECEIVERS BECAUSE NOT EVEN THE GOOD UP GOOD UP LIFE HE GOOD GOD AND ALLELUJAH HAS GIVEN US WE CAN TAKE CARE OF.

By now you know if you are walking on the right path to Good God and he truly loves you, HE will do all to save you, so that you do not walk on a dirty road. He's doing this with me. And it's weird not funny, how I wanted a drink and did not drink. My sons went to work downtown Toronto, and on their way to work they saw someone get hit by a bike. She was flown into the air. She was so drunk my son said that she walked into the road, and when someone wanted to call the police she did not want them to.

Yes Satan proved his point and because of the lies of humans, Satan laughs at Good God because he achieved his objective. HE SATAN TURNED GOOD GOD'S CHILDREN AGAINST HIM. HE USED GREED, RELIGION AND HUE TO MANIPULATE AND DECEIVE.

Not one of us can blame Good God for this but I do because I can, I've made him my all. As humans we were told in the Book of Sin what Satan was going to do and instead of stopping Satan, we gave him the victory over us daily. So the debt load that humans have racked up over the past 24000 years is so great that millions if not billions of you are going to spend trillions of years in hell burning worse than a bitch in heat for your sins.

I've told you in some of my other books that I've seen heaven and hell and they are side by side. The people in hell are trying to get into heaven right now and can't because there is no one there to save them.

ALL OF YOU ARE RELYING ON JESUS TO SAVE YOU, BUT GOOD GOD'S CHILDREN; THE ONES TO SAVE YOU ARE NOT MALES, THEY ARE FEMALES. AND LIKE I'VE TOLD YOU, IF I AM THE SAVING GRACE FOR HUMANITY I WILL NEVER EVER WITHOUT DOUBT SAVE ANYONE THAT IS WICKED AND EVIL. YOU KNOW THE EVILS THAT YOU DID AND DO, SO TRULY PAY FOR THEM. IT IS NOT FAIR FOR YOU TO KILL AND CAUSE PAIN WITHOUT BEING PUNISHED, HENCE "THE WAGES OF SIN IS DEATH." YOU DID WRONG AND

INSTEAD OF CLEANING UP YOURSELF YOU WANT SOMEONE TO DIE AND BURN IN HELL FOR YOU.

WHY THE HELL SHOULD SOMEONE DIE TO SAVE YOUR WICKED AND EVIL ASS?

WHO THE HELL ARE YOU TO THINK YOUR LIFE IS WORTH MORE THAN THE NEXT MAN OR WOMAN; CHILD?

WHO THE HELL ARE YOU TO THINK YOU ARE BETTER THAN THE NEXT MAN OR WOMAN; CHILD.

YOU DID WRONG; CLEAN YOUR MESS UP COME ON NOW.

YOU SINNED AND I'M TO GIVE UP MY LIFE FOR YOU!!!

WHAT ABOUT THE LIFE OF MY CHILDREN; FAMILY; THE FAMILY HE GOOD GOD AND ALLELUJAH HAS AND HAVE GIVEN ME?

WHEN I GIVE UP MY LIFE FOR YOU, WHAT ABOUT THEM?

WHO IS GOING TO SAVE THEM?

When they are in need where are you going to be? Come on tell me. So why the hell would Good God commission anyone to die for you?

How fair are you?
You were not fair to others on earth but yet you seek a saving grace from death in the end. <u>LET ME TELL YOU THIS, DEATH LET'S NO ONE GO JUST LIKE THAT COME ON NOW.</u> I OF ALL PEOPLE KNOW THIS. I KNOW THE REALM OF DEATH AND WHAT DEATH WILL DO TO KEEP ALL WICKED AND SINFUL IN HIS FOLD. SO WHY THE HELL WOULD I CONTINUE TO PISS OFF FEMALE DEATH?

<u>I TRULY REFUSE TO SAVE ANY OF YOU.</u> DO GOOD AND GOOD WILL FOLLOW YOU. YOU DO NOT HURT PEOPLE AND THINK IT IS GOING TO BE OKAY. THIS IS WHY HELL WAS CREATED. HELL AND OR THE DEVIL AND OR DEATH MUST GET THEIR PAY AND THEIR PAY IS RIGHTFULLY YOU BECAUSE YOU WILLINGLY AND KNOWINGLY SINNED. DEATH CANNOT SAVE YOU, DEATH CAN

ONLY KILL YOU AND EVERYONE KNOWS THIS, BUT YET BILLIONS FOLLOW DEATH ANYWAY; THEN HAVE THE GAUL TO SAY SOMEONE IS GOING TO DIE TO SAVE THEM.

<u>NO ONE CAN DIE TO SAVE YOU; YOU HAVE TO LIVE TO SAVE YOU COME ON NOW.</u>

YOU KILLED RECKLESS AND RUDE ON EARTH AND NOW YOU WANT A SAVING GRACE; WHAT GAUL.

TAKE A GOOD AND TRUE LOOK AT THE LIVES YOU'VE TAKEN OVER THE CENTURIES.

TAKE A GOOD LOOK AT THE LIVES YOU'VE TAKEN IN THIS DAY AND TIME.

TAKE A GOOD AND TRUE LOOK AT THE WEAPONS AND DISEASES YOU CREATED TO KILL ANOTHER HUMAN BEING.

TAKE A GOOD AND TRUE LOOK AT THE SLAVERY; THE BRUTALITY YOU THE WHITE RACE HAS AND HAVE INFLICTED ON THE BLACK MAN AND JEWS.

TAKE A GOOD AND TRUE LOOK AT THE DEATH TOLL AND TELL ME WHY SHOULD ANYONE SAVE A HATEFUL AND SPITEFUL RACE OF PEOPLE LIKE YOU BASED ON HUE?

<u>YOU KILLED AND NOW YOU WANT IN.</u>

LOOK AT THE DISEASES YOU CREATED AND SPREAD; THEN LIE TO HUMANITY AND SAY THESE DISEASES CAME FROM THE BLACK RACE WHEN YOU DESIGNED AND CREATED THEM IN YOUR LABORATORIES. SO NOW TELL ME; <u>WHY THE HELL SHOULD ANYONE BLACK SAVE YOUR MURDEROUS ASSES?</u>

YOU DESIGN TO KILL BUT YET LIE ON ANOTHER RACE, SO WHY THE HELL SHOULD GOOD GOD AND ALLELUJAH SAVE YOU WHEN YOU HAVE NOT MERCY; TRUE LOVE IN YOUR HEARTS.

YOU ARE VILE MURDERERS HENCE SHE CURSED YOUR ASS FOR THE VILENESS YOU DO.

<u>I know for a fact Good God and Allelujah will never ever let anyone die to save wicked and evil; sinful and vile people.</u> This is why in your book of sin, Psalms One say in part, "blessed is the man that walketh not in the council of the ungodly nor sitteth in the seat of the scornful."

We've read this Psalms and some of us know this Psalms by heart, but yet we do otherwise anyway.

Yes it's April 21, 2015 and the dreams are coming more and more because THERE IS SOMETHING I AM MISSING WITH THE WHITE RACE BASED ON HUE.

I keep missing the plane and bus when it comes to the White Race and Good God is showing me this. This is not the first time I've been missing the White Race because they are at the second level of the mountain of Good God and Allelujah.

Maybe I am reading the mountain wrong in my interpretations hence missing my mark when it comes to the White Race based on hue and hue only.

Level one of the mountain   **Blacks and Chinese**

Level two of the mountain   **Whites Only**
Level three of the mountain   **Blacks Only**

Level Two is where you get protection as well because the dead do protect some in the living.

So Good God and Allelujah what am I missing because I am missing something and this something you need humanity to know about.

Fam, I've been dreaming about White People more and more based on hue not deeds. Dreamt I was in this building. It's a place I know because I lived there. (Malton)

I was walking in the hall because apparently I was seeking a place to live and they had four bedroom units. Going back to the building and or condo at the time when I lived there I saw lots of white children running in the hallway. The hallway had decorated carpet of red and other colours; truly lovely. Seeing the kids I wondered where they came from. As I walked by them there was this Babylonian lady passing me and I am pretty sure I did not greet her. Older white people lived in the building and I wondered if the noise disturbed them but don't quote me on this. I ended up going to the front of the building where the elevators were and two elevators opened up and all you saw was white people scrambling to fill up the elevator on the right. I ended up in the elevator on the left. I pressed floor number 6 and ended up getting on this bus for which I was lost. I don't know how I ended up on the bus with this white female driver but I did. I thought she would take me to my apartment but it was the wrong bus I was on. I had to get off and take another bus. I ended up in another vehicle and sat at the back of this car. I had my brown and grey floral throw on me. The car stopped and picked up these two young black gentleman and one of them in grey pants sat on my throw for which irritated me. I had to pull my throw from under him because he was in his dirty work clothes. Getting off at a location I saw this young black girl who was in blue jeans (don't quote me on the blue jeans) but she had a blue pants on and I think yellow shirt and hat; tam. She was saying she went to Jamaica and she caught Chicken Gunya (Chick V) or Chicken Virus. She said it's going to take 3 months to get the virus fully out of her system and I told it's going to take 7 years to get the virus out of her system.

She was saying as she walked to her destination that she thought that they brought Chicken Gunya to Jamaica to infect the people and I asked her why Jamaica. Jamaica was the only Caribbean Island that had such a bad outbreak. I told her from I was growing up I've never heard of mosquitoes infecting anyone and nuff mosquito bit us up when we were growing up. I also asked her, why not the Cayman Islands? But they could not affect and infect the Cayman Islands due to Cayman having more banks per capita than people. So as I journeyed on I took this long dirt road and the two men in the car with me was behind me playing and or doing their antics until they passed me. Rushed by me. One of them saw this car and it was his dream car. People this car I've never seen in my life before. It's like something out of a sci-fi movie. It's as if the car had feathers, black feathers to me but there was no feathers. The car is black, very black and it was long like those armoured vehicles but it wasn't. It had bars on the back of it because these two guys hopped on the back of the car and held on to the bars as they joyride to their destination which was a church because you could hear the church music going and they hopped off in glee and excited rush. (Sorry for the run on sentence).

No, I did not go into the church because you had to cross the road to get to the church and I did not cross the road, I just saw in my walk what was happening. Oh I forgot, when I went into the elevator I had my white shirt on, (my son's shirt that I wear to bed) on and it had a stain on the shirt. So weird dream and I am so going to leave this dream alone because like I said, I keep missing the plane and bus when it comes to the White Race based on hue.

I also dreamt I was with the musical group Morgan Heritage back home. I can't tell you all about the dream. All I know was that they were chasing me and other

Rastas was chasing me (Jah Cure). People, this dream is so odd because I had bread, ½ loaf of white bread and I had it in my hand and dem a run mi dung. Yes in the end they got the bread, cut it up and was eating the bread. In the dream the bread seemed a bit hard but was edible. After they got the bread, I ended up in this home with Morgan Heritage and I was talking to this black lady. I cannot describe her to you, all I can remember vaguely is that she had low cut black hair but do not quote me on the low cut black hair, but she did have low cut hair. I cannot tell you what we were talking about because I cannot truly remember. She was not fat or skinny but medium built. This was dream number one. But this dream started off in space but I cannot fully tell you about the space part. All I know is fighting, WHITE PEOPLE FIGHTING. <u>**No, I swear this is all white people based on hue can do. Fight and kill.**</u>

EVERY FIGHT I SEE IN THE UNIVERSE AND OR ON OTHER PLANETS, A PURE WHITE PEOPLE. WHAT THE HELL DO YOU PEOPLE HAVE TO FIGHT ABOUT?

WHY CAN'T THE FIGHTING STOP WITH YOU PEOPLE? WHAT THE HELL ARE YOU FIGHTING FOR?
Hell is there and you know the wages of sin is death, but yet you keeping locking yourself out of Good God's world and kingdom; abode. How dumb can you be?

BUT THEN I SHOULD NOT WONDER OR PONDER BECAUSE SHE DID PUT A CURSE ON YOUR RACE. YOU ARE TO FIGHT AND KILL FOR EVERYTHING HENCE YOUR CURSE IS BOTH PHYSICAL AND SPIRITUAL.

YOU CANNOT LIVE IN HARMONY AND OR PEACE WITH ANYONE BECAUSE THIS IS ALL YOU KNOW. HENCE ARIES THE GOD OF WAR. THE FIRST SIGN OF YOUR ZODIAC. YOU ARE WARMONGERS THAT CANNOT STOP LOOTING AND FIGHTING; KILLING BECAUSE PEACE IS TRULY NOT WITH YOUR RACE AT ALL AND THIS IS A CRYING SHAME. Yes people this is a crying shame. Instead of breaking her spell you continue to fight and kill.

<u>MAYBE</u> THIS IS WHAT GOOD GOD IS TRYING IS TRYING TO TELL ME.

<u>MAYBE</u> HE'S TRYING TO TELL ME THAT THE WHITE RACE BASED ON HUE; YOU;

CANNOT BE SAVED. YOU THE WHITE RACE IS TOO VILE AND WICKED; SINFUL.

MAYBE GOOD GOD IS SAYING TO YOU THE WHITE RACE, BECAUSE I REFUSE TO SAVE WICKED AND EVIL PEOPLE, NOT ONE OF YOU WILL BE SAVED IF I AM THE SAVING GRACE FOR HUMANITY.

MAYBE HE GOOD GOD IS TELLING ME THAT ALL WHITE PEOPLE ARE LOCKED OUT OF HIS KINGDOM AND ABODE, BECAUSE SHE, YOUR OWN WHITE CURSED YOU LONG BEFORE ADAM AND EVE.

MAYBE HE GOOD GOD AND ALLELUJAH IS TELLING ME THAT YOU ARE THE CURSED RACE AND NOTHING THAT YOU DO WILL OR CAN SAVE YOU.

SO IN KNOWING THIS WHITE PEOPLE WHAT ARE YOU TRULY GOING TO DO?

How are you going to get into Good God's kingdom based on HUE AND YOUR HATRED FOR EVERYONE AND EVERYTHING NON WHITE?

I truly do not want to be any of you because hell is waiting for the lots of you. Remember, <u>you design to kill and do kill.</u>

You've murdered and enslaved many in your time here on earth and many of you carry generational curses; sins. So truly good luck to the lots of you when Black Death comes for you and hand your asses over to White Death for sentencing; your death. Don't worry a lot of black people will join you; change to become white as snow. Hence the bleaching some already do in the living.

WOW BECAUSE I TRULY DO NOT FEEL SORRY FOR BILLIONS OF YOU. <u>**NOPE BECAUSE PAYBACK IS TRULY A BITCH.**</u> **HENCE BILLIONS OF YOU ARE GOING TO BURN FOR THE SINS AND WRONGS YOU HAVE DONE TO HUMANITY, THE ANIMAL KINGDOM, EARTH AND THE ENVIRONMENT.** *Like I said, you do not hurt people and think the bullshit that you do you are going to get away with it.* **So yes, Good God you did good and well unto your own because billions are truly locked out of your world and kingdom for real.**

And yes people I know what I did. Hence I based things above on hue not deeds. Good and true people; White People know that the classification above does not GOVERN THEM. THEY ARE GOOD AND TRUE.

GOOD AND TRUE PEOPLE DO NOT HURT EACH OTHER. THEY HAVE GOODNESS AND RESPECT FOR EACH OTHER. THE CLASSIFICATION ABOVE GOES FOR THE WICKED AND EVIL THAT FALLS UNDER THE WHITE BANNER; DEATH.

No, truly please don't because Good God does not base anything on hue in the living like I've told you. I had to do this for you to think, well the White Race to think. You cannot base life on hue; you have to base life on goodness and truth. And hey, I have to be just and true because I have white blood in me. Hence I have to be just and fair to all in all that I do. Many things I cannot change, hence I will not change the law that governs the true Jews. Nor will I change the law that governs many black people who have died accepting Islam like my mother. They truly did not know the truth, so I have to save those good black people that wanted and needed better for self. They did not know that if they accepted Islam they were accepting spiritual death. So yes the saving grace still stands for them. Provisions were made for them and it would be wicked of me to change this. There are things we do not know in life and if a good door has been opened by Good God for these people, who am I to close it?

Many the devil fooled, hence **FOOLS DIE FOR WANT OF WISDOM Peter Tosh.** Truly listen to this song because if we do not clean up self and this earth now, we will all be doomed. Yes many of you can stay your death, but you have to want to live. And with all that is happening here on earth right now, truly good luck because *I KNOW MANY OF YOU ARE LAUGHING AT ME AND CALLING ME A FOOL. HENCE IT MATTERS NOT WHAT YOU THINK OF ME BECAUSE I DID RELAY THE MESSAGES OF GOOD GOD BACK TO YOU AND YOU IGNORED HIM AND ME. YOU WERE THE IGNORANT ONES THAT LIVE FOR LIES AND DECEIT.*

Hey Noah did his job in your book of sin and I've done mine. **So if I am the only one to be saved, then yeah me and better for me. So yes I will be the one to say Abay, kiss it bitches, you were told and your ignorant self did not listen.** Trust me as soon as Good God say, Michelle gather, di door done shut. He

Good God nuh affi finish im sentence. <u>Our door will be impenetrable to all who are locked out because I know what's coming.</u> Every arsenal of death here on earth will be unleashed on humanity. When Good God's people are safe in the lands he needs them to be in, truly good luck to the rest of you because Death will take you literally. So no, I truly do not worry about wicked and evil people at all because there's an app for them, and that app is hell literally. *So truly listen to FOOLS DIE FOR WANT OF WISDOM by Peter Tosh because he did tell you and warn you.* He did his part in spreading the message of Good God. And for all of you that's going to come around me and say give me your power and teach me what you know so that I can save many, truly do not come because **GOOD GOD GIVETH KNOWLEDGE NOT ME.** <u>**I am just his child and writer.**</u> If you want his knowledge go to him directly and ask him to give you his knowledge. And for you that are going to come with the I am going to test you bullshit. <u>**TRULY DON'T.**</u> **TAKE A LOOK AT THE INTERNET AND SEE HOW JAMAICANS CUSS OUT PEOPLE WICKED AND RUDE WHEN PROVOKED. I AM NO DIFFERENT, BECAUSE MI A CUSSA FROM MI BAANE, SO TRULY DON'T TRY IT WITH ME BECAUSE A MORE DAN YOU MUMMA MI WI CUSS.**

SO YOU ARE DULY WARNED.

I also dreamt this Babylonian Muslim family, they were walking and I was walking and I cannot remember what happened, but I think the child said something to me and I had to put him in his place. *I told him "HE SHOULD GO BACK TO WHERE HE CAME FROM." I also told him I am not a murderer, I am not the one to walk and murder people they were.*

Did the father and or family take me on?

They couldn't say a thing; hence I went my way in true peace. Those are all the dreams I can remember for this morning. Oh even though I did not see this dream this morning. I dreamt Bob Marley this week. I believe it was Sunday morning as it's Tuesday. I dreamt Cedella Marley. She went into her father's grave and or tomb and she came out crying. You could see her in tears, so I have to watch and see if anyone is going to die in this family soon.

I also dreamt, I was at my grandmother's home in Jamaica and these Indian Babylonians stopped off at her gate. This one man started to tell lies. Not on me but his own Babylonian female because he was male. People I had to put him in his place with his lies. I told him he's a liar and he's telling lies. Hence I have to ask, **what does it profit a man to tell lies and send his soul and or spirit to hell to be burned? If you know the truth, tell the truth and save yourself not lie and die. Come on now.**

MY TALK – BOOK FIVE

So like I said, I truly do not know what Good God and Allelujah is trying to show me when it comes to WHITE PEOPLE AND OR THE WHITE RACE.

I know White People, Black People can save you; let you in because we are of the same lineage; race and we share the same blood and life line. SEE THE YING AND YANG FOR CLARIFICATION. You know what, let me embed the Ying and Yang for you to see for some of you ignorant people that won't know what I am writing and or talking about.

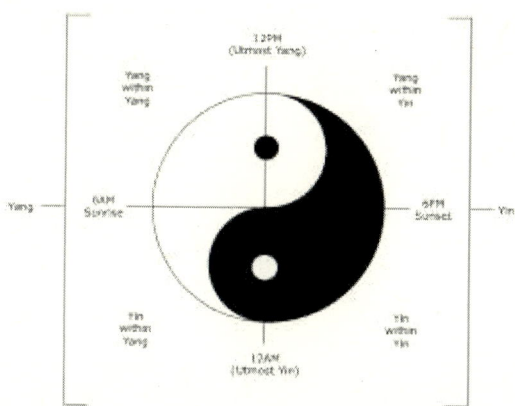

And yes I chose the one with time on purpose. Hence there is no difference between the Whites and Blacks a part from hue. Hence some whites are black and some blacks are white. It is self explanatory. **Hence YOU HAVE BLACK AND WHITE DEATH. THEY WORK IN UNISON TOGETHER; HENCE DEATH CANNOT CHANGE. DEATH MUST REMAIN THE SAME IN ALL ASPECT OF LIFE; WELL DEATH.**

Yes I have many questions to ask Good God but I have to wonder why?

Why you White People based on hue?

You kill without remorse.
You design and create diseases to kill.
You kill your own and others.
HENCE DEATH COMES THROUGH YOU AND ONLY YOU NOT THE TRUE BLACK RACE.

Your skin tone already say it all.

Go back to Abraham when he put his hand in his chest and when he withdrew it, it became leprous as snow.

So you are cursed, were the cursed race but yet you tell others otherwise.

<u>And no I truly do not want to spread hate, but I have to wonder if GOOD GOD AND ALLELUJAH IS TRYING TO TELL ME THAT YOU, THE ENTIRE WHITE POPULATION BASED ON HUE IS LOCKED OUT INFINITELY AND INDEFINITELY FOREVER EVER WITHOUT END OUT OF HIS KINGDOM AND ABODE.</u>

Is this his way of telling me that the WHITE RACE BASED ON HUE, HAVE NO CHANCE IN HELL TO GET INTO HIS KINGDOM AND ABODE. YOU ARE ALL HELL BOUND BECAUSE OF YOUR MURDEROUS AND EVIL TENDANCIES; WAYS AND CULTURE.

If this is so, then truly good luck to the lots of you because my word stand for more than infinite and indefinite lifetimes and generations to come more than forever ever without end when I say, I WILL NEVER EVER WITHOUT END SAVE ANYONE THAT IS WICKED AND EVIL. YOUR RACE BASED ON HUE NOT DEEDS, HAVE AND HAS DONE ENOUGH WICKEDNESS TO ALL OF HUMANITY THAT NOTHING THAT ANY OF YOU DO CAN SAVE YOU.

From the spiritual realm to the earthly realm you fight and kill and take what truly do not belong to you. Hence you are the true Sikh and or sickly race. Everywhere you go you bring disease and sickness; sin and the ultimate; DEATH and not one of you has or have tried to stop this and change your nasty and filthy ways.

Yes you are seen on the mountain of Good God, but what's the point of being separated from the rest of the mountain?

What's the point of doing all the evils that you do for a place in hell? **SHE CONDEMNED YOU BECAUSE OF YOUR WARLIKE MENTALITY AND THE KILLINGS THAT YOU DO. YOU HAVE A CHANCE TO CHANGE THIS BUT YOU REFUSE TO. INSTEAD YOU JOIN THE BABYLONIAN RACE AND CONTINUE TO CONDEMN SELF AND WORLD.**

So yes, when it comes to you, I am missing something. ***HE GOOD GOD IS TRYING TO TELL YOU SOMETHING. HE IS TRYING TO TELL YOU THAT YOU CAN BE SAVED BUT IT'S UP TO YOU TO PUT DOWN YOUR MURDEROUS TENDANCIES AND LIVE.*** *Walk right and do all that is right to save you. We know that spiritual death looks like you, and it matters not if you are Black, White, Chinese or Indian. When spiritual wickedness dies and or the physical wicked that is here on earth dies and or when they shed the flesh, they die as white and dressed in white in the*

spiritual world. ***SO WHEN PEOPLE TELL ME ABOUT WHITE JESUS AND SHOW ME WHITE JESUS, THEY ARE SHOWING ME SPIRITUAL DEATH IN ITS NATURAL FORM. I KNOW JESUS IS DEATH AND IT MATTERS NOT IF HE IS WHITE OR BLACK. BLACK JESUS REPRESENTS PHYSICAL DEATH, THE PERSON WHO TAKES THE SPIRIT FROM ITS PRISON THE FLESH. BLACK DEATH CANNOT KILL ONLY WHITE DEATH CAN AND IT IS WHITE DEATH WHO KILLS THE SPIRIT LITERALLY. HENCE AS IT IS IN HEAVEN SO IT IS ON EARTH. YES DEATH KILLS IN HEAVEN AND DEATH KILLS ON EARTH HENCE PHYSICAL AND SPIRITUAL DEATH.***
Many of you do not know this and for many of you yes, I am repeating myself because like I said, I am missing something when it comes to you the White Race based on hue not deeds.

Brother cannot continue to kill brother because the White Race did come out of Black Loins; Genes. Hence you can more than over stand and comprehend Albinism. You were told in your book of sin that Noah curse the first seed of Ham which is Canaan. But in my vision of old, it was not Noah that cursed you the White Race, it was a woman; your own kind that cursed you. **AND YOUR CURSE HAD NOTHING TO DO WITH THE PHYSICAL REALM INITIALLY IT HAD TO DO WITH THE SPIRITUAL REALM.** *You were not a part of the original creation hence the bullshit with Satan coming to earth and creating havoc.* YOU WERE WITH GOD, BUT NO, YOU WANTED MORE FROM READING YOUR BOOK OF SIN. INSTEAD OF FINDING YOUR TRUE PLACE, YOU TURNED WARMONGERS AND MURDERERS THAT RAPE AND STEAL, BRING DEATH EVERYWHERE YOU DAMN WELL GO AND FOR WHAT?

Good God never denied you access to him. **THUS YOU HAVE GOOD AND EVIL; THE WHITE AND THE BLACK RACE BASED ON DEEDS, YES GOOD AND EVIL NOT HUE. BUT I HAD TO BRING HUE INTO THIS BECAUSE YOU BASE ALL ON HUE AND NOT ON THE GOOD AND TRUTH THAT YOU DO. HENCE NOT ALL WHITES ARE WHITE SOME ARE BLACK. MEANING SOME FALL UNDER THE BLACK BANNER AND THIS IS WHY IT IS PERMISSIBLE FOR THE BLACK RACE BASED ON DEEDS (GOODNESS AND TRUTH) TO MARRY THEIR OWN WHITE KIND BASED ON DEEDS – GOODNESS AND**

TRUTH AND NOT ON HUE AND OR BASED ON HUE.

Good God cannot base anything off hue. **HE MUST BASE EVERYTHING OFF AND OR ON TRUTH; GOODNESS AND TRUTH.** SO THE HATRED MUST STOP AND STOP TODAY IF YOU WANT BACK YOUR PLACE AND SPACE WITH HIM GOOD GOD. YOU CANNOT FIGHT FOR THE DEVIL BECASUE YOU DO NOT BELONG TO THE DEVIL; **HENCE THE UNIVERSE IS A MIXTURE OF RACE.** THE UNIVERSE IS BOTH BLACK AND WHITE; BIRACIAL FOR SOME. I'VE TOLD YOU THIS IN ANOTHER BOOK, SO TRULY TELL ME WHAT THE HELL ARE YOU AGAINST THE BLACK RACE FOR? WHY THE HELL DO YOU FIGHT WHEN YOU CAN BREAK THE CHAIN OF THIS CURSE? And why are you the Black Race fighting against your white counterparts. You are damn well family and you fight against your own. If we did not sin originally then the hue bullshit would not come into play. **WE CARRY THE SIN GENE JUST LIKE THE WHITE RACE CARRY THE BLACK GENE. WE ARE EACH OTHER'S OPPOSITES DUMB DUMB.**

Look at what she did to me. I over came her because in death she needed my forgiveness and I truly did not give it to her. She is not deserving of it. She did me wrong and I will never ever without end forgive her for this because I did her nothing. And like I said, I refuse to save anyone that is wicked and evil because you that are wicked and evil know what you are doing. You know you are causing pain and suffering, so why should anyone that is good and true save you?

You are not deserving of a saving grace, hence I refuse to do anything based on hue because I know our hue and or skin tone is bullshit from a life and death stand point.

True life is not based on hue. Hence Good and True people will always be saved. You as an individual have your own life in your hands, so live it good and true. **Put down the hurt and killing bullshit because all this does is get you into hell literally.**

Maybe this is what He Good God wants me to tell you the white race and it's up to you to listen. **SO TRULY DON'T COME TO ME WITH YOUR BLACK OR WHITE SUPERIORITY BULLSHIT BECAUSE I WILL TELL YOU WHERE TO STICK IT AND HOW TO ROTATE ON IT.**

Take your White Crap and Black Crap bullshit someplace else. And yes I will not get down on the Chinese Race because they were the only smart ones in the lots of you. They accepted life long ago; hence they kept the Ying and Yang true. Many have not strayed from it.

No, we are not to worship the Ying Yang because this is life and it's also death. Hence death is not on the first and third level of the mountain of Good God, it's on the second level. <u>So as we pass through life, many must face death due to sin.</u>

The righteous and pure at heart cannot face death because they are not governed by death. Death cannot stop true life; hence these people and or spirits by pass this stage in life and go straight to the top. They must go up to see Good God and Allelujah, hence the upright eye in triangle. See every nation plays a part in the sequence of life; things. Many nations listen to foolish people (based on religion) tell them bullshit about death. BUT DEATH CANNOT SAVE ANYONE, DEATH CAN ONLY TAKE THEM AND OR KILL THEM AND I'VE TOLD YOU THIS TIME AND TIME AGAIN. Good God and Allelujah do not deal in death, he gives life; true and good life. Life cannot take life only death can. This is the job of death hence the devil has his race of people that manipulate and kill, take life in the living. Like I said, she cursed you the White Race and it's through you that diseases come. You are a set of people that like (s) to war and create havoc everywhere you go and I truly do not know why. **You cannot kill to live; you can only kill to die.**

And you the White Race are going to die. The lives you take and has taken have you and your children locked in hell but some of you are saved because like I said, not all Whites are Whites; some of you fall under the Black Banner hence you are Black. Like I've said this is not based on hue (skin tone) but based on deeds; the good that you do and the truth that you live. **Once you get your upright eye in triangle you are saved, you have to move up to see Good God and Allelujah literally.** Hence America, the United States of America, you had true and good life and lost it. You gave up your place with Good God to fight with the devil's seed. They have you fighting while you racked up a national debt that you cannot repay. You also delivered your people into the hands of death and nothing that you do can or will save them because death has you, yes your land and people literally. The devil knew what he was doing, hence he lied to you. You had life literally (the life you had was the life the devil wanted and if he could not get it, he was going to destroy you) and you threw it away. Hence I told you, Life came to Life and Life rejected Life. Yes Marcus Mosiah Garvey. You did not listen to him and look at America today. Poor and destitute and it's only going to get worse for the lots of you. You did not listen to the truth hence your life must come to an end real soon. Pity.

Onwards I Go

You have to shed the hue of flesh in the spirit because NO ONE CAN TAKE HUE (COLOUR OF SKIN) TO GOOD GOD BECAUSE TRUE LIFE HATH NO HUE. Hence the hue of man is baseless and hath no merit when it comes to life, but it hath merit when it comes to death. Everything that you do is written down and is read out to you at death. Hence death has your name and number. **THE NUMBER IS THE TIME YOU WILL SPEND IN HELL BURNING. HENCE THE NUMBER OF SIN AND OR DEATH IS NOT 18, IT IS 24.**

666 FOR SOME, BUT FOR THOSE WHO TRULY KNOW, IT'S <u>6666</u>.

666 REPRESENTS THE 3 DAUGHTERS SATAN HAD WITH EVE (EVENING); BUT IN YOUR BOOK OF BEGINNINGS (GENESIS) CAIN, ABEL AND SETH REPRESENTS THESE GIRLS. Yes this is for those who know the full truth. 6666 represents the 3 daughters of Satan and Satan himself, hence 3XY in mathematical equation; 3 females to 1 male.

In the spiritual realm it's 2yx. Meaning whenever male and female spirits walk you have 2 males to one female. The female walks in the middle not the outer. So there is one male to the right and left of that female. Yes you can have 3y. 3y is total destruction of land and people. A messenger or child of Good God and Allelujah can stop this death if they are ordained to do so. <u>Hence it's imperative to know the spiritual realm because all is not what it seems.</u>

Yes I've strayed because I am being repetitive in this book big time and no I am not looking for fillers.

I need to talk to you the WHITE RACE AND I TRULY DO NOT KNOW WHAT TO SAY TO YOU. I still cannot comprehend why you would continue to kill and deceive instead of BREAKING HER SPELL AND LIVE.

WHY DO YOU HAVE TO KILL TO DIE?

When you kill you lock yourself out of Good God's true kingdom and abode and I cannot understand why?

Why do you have to kill and die?

Why fight for Aries and continue with the trend of death?

Wow I feel it because this did not have to be this way. You cannot take on the realm of death, meaning continue to kill for a place in hell because no one deserves to die. From the beginning until now you've been fighting, murdering and enlisting others in your bloodbath and it has to stop.

NO ONE CAN FIGHT FOR THE TRUTH BECAUSE THE TRUTH DOES NOT FIGHT. ONCE EVERYTHING IS OVER THE TRUTH MUST BE REVEALED NO MATTER HOW LONG IT TAKES. ABSOLUTELY NO ONE CAN HIDE FROM THE TRUTH.

We all know the "wages of sin is death," but yet we sin anyway and this is wrong on all levels.

No one can take their sins and or evils to Good God and we all know this. The death trend must to stop. 24 thousand years hath you to change your dirty and sinful ways and you've done nothing to stop this. **SO**

BECAUSE OF THIS, THE EXTINCTION OF MAN COMES BEFORE 2032. YOU LIVED FOR DEATH AND DO ALL FOR DEATH, SO DEATH MUST TAKE YOU BECAUSE YOU GAVE YOUR LIVES OVER TO DEATH. Thus saith the Lord thy God meaning it is so.

You cannot say you want and need life AND TAKE AWAY FROM THE BREATH OF LIFE. (Good God and Allelujah). Come on now.

You cannot say you are going to see Good God and Allelujah when BLOOD IS IN AND ON YOUR HANDS.

There are generational sins and if you have not made amends for them, YOU AND YOUR ANCESTORS CANNOT BE SAVED. You should all know this.

Yes each race, no not all race have a lifeline with Good God and Allelujah and you should know this.

LIFE IS NOT SUPERIOR TO LIFE BECAUSE LIFE IS LIFE. TRUE LIFE IS GOOD AND TRUE, BUT EVIL LIFE IS DEATH OF THE SELF AND SPIRIT INCLUDING THE ENVIRONMENT YOU LIVE IN.

None of us can say we know not the truth because we do. We just refuse to accept it and we refuse to live by the truth.

We would rather live in lies and die rather than live in truth and live.

You have a chance to save yourself now, so truly take your lifeline and live. He Good God is giving you one (a chance to live) so truly do the right thing. Yes you may have many concerns, but do like I do, bug him Good God.

Don't you dare tell me no. Bug him for the truth. Yes bug him about me too. **Hey, you don't have to trust me but trust him because He Good God will never lead you astray.**

Yes you can call me a liar and this is up to you. But would a liar tell you to save yourself? Would a liar face hell to tell you to live good and clean?

But I have to give up my lifestyle, I love going to parties you are saying.

So go to your parties; no one is stopping you from having fun. Go out with your girlfriend or male friends, but the picking up thing and whoredom you cannot do.

I truly love music hence I listen to all kinds of music. No not all kinds of music because I truly don't like Babylonian Music, nor do I like some of the dancehall crap that's being phished on the internet.

And to get off track here, Jamaica what the hell are you doing to self? No not Jamaica but the people of Jamaica.

Yes di cussing start now because some a unnu need fi cuss wuse dan drangcrow.

Was watching some of the fights on the internet and You DI YOUNG WUKLESS AND CARELESS GYAL WEY CHUCK DI OLE OMAN DUNG, NOA SEY BAD BLESSING TEK YOU, DEY PAN YU. It matters not how vile and wicked this woman is to you. Under no circumstances are you to put your hands on an old person no matter what you think of her. Yu cuss har an sey yu peace, lef har. Yes shi up inna yu face but walk away from har, shi ole and shi ha fi har owna waterloo to face in di grave. Hence some of the people (younger generation) of Jamaica have and has become vile and disgusting.

An fi unnu nasty scumbags wey put di video of the young lady fighting without clothes and a tek picture of har, truly hope NONE A UNNU NUH HA PICKNEY BECAUSE RETRIBUTION IS A BITCH WHEN IT COMES AROUND. TAKE THAT DISGUSTING SHIT DOWN FROM OFF THE INTERNET. NO WONDER OTHER NATIONS CAN CALL US ANIMALS. AND NOT EVEN ANIMALS ACT AS DISGUSTING AS SOME OF YOU.

AND I AM GOING TO GO OFF WORSE NOW. AND FOR YOU DI WHORING JESIBEL WEY HA YU PICKNEY A CUSS OUT ANOTHER CHILD RUDE AND RECKLESS, YOU ARE NOT A MOTHER. YOU ARE WORSE THAN A GHETTO TROLL AN HOG THAT SHOULD NOT HAVE CHILDREN. YOU ARE EGGING ON YOUR CHILD TO CUSS SUH. YOU ARE MORE THAN DISGUSTING; HENCE YOU STINK WORSE THAN A DECOMPOSING BODY. YOU ARE THE EPIDEMY OF STENCH AND NO MAN SHOULD LAY WITH FILTH OF WORSE THAN STENCH LIKE YOU. HENCE THE STENCH SOME A UNNU AS PARENTS TEACH THEM; YOUR CHILDREN. THUS THE APPLE TRULY DOESN'T FALL FAR FROM THE WHORING AND DECOMPOSING TREE. UNNU MEK MI OLE MI HEAD DUNG INNA SHAME. HENCE NUH BETTA BARREL NUH BETTA BLEEPING HERRING.

ALL DI SCUMBAGS WEY DO DI SHIT TO DI OLE MAN. DI MAN DRUNK AND HIM WIFE AND OR OMAN A TRY FI TEK HIM HOME AND UNNU A EGG DI MAN ON FI DRINK MORE. WHAT IF DI MAN DI FALL DOWN AND DEAD? OR WHAT IF

IM DID FALL DUNG AN HURT IMSELF? WHAT WOULD YOU SAY? BLEEPING DISGUSTING. MEMBA SEY UNNU A GET OLE AND WHAT GOES AROUND COMES AROUND. HENCE RETRIBUTION SOON TEK UNNU AND IF EEE NUH TEK UNNU, LOOK PAN EEE PICKNEY INNA UNNU HAN. HENCE OLE PEOPLE SEY WHAT DROP OFFA HEAD DROP PAN SHOULDER. SO WHEN RETRIBUTION TEK YU PICKNEY DO NOT COMPLAIN AND SAY GOOD GOD AND OR PEOPLE WICKED BECAUSE YOUR ACTIONS WAS WHAT CONDEMNED YOU. BLEEPING DISGUSTING.

<u>No wonder my second son sey mama technology a guh kill wi.</u> Instead of becoming our brothers and sisters keeper we've become their disgrace and shame; murderers and killers. No people, I am tired of the shame and disgrace on the internet now man come on now. **<u>Is this what our forefathers fought so damned hard for? Fi unnu fi come out and shame self.</u>** Yes mi cuss unnu but the anger is there and some a unnu need fi cuss. I am not perfect nor am I a model citizen but some shit we as humans do can stop and we should not do.

AS BLACK PEOPLE WE ARE THE ONES SHAMING EACH OTHER. AND YES YOU CAN SAY I DO THE SAME TOO WITH MY CUSSING IN SOME OF THESE BOOKS. But come on now, think of your actions and what you are doing. Some of you have family, sisters and brothers. I am sure if it's your sister or a family member you would not like it. Think because disrespect is disrespect.

Yes you may say I disrespectful and need a cussing myself, hence I have to try to do better with the cussing. I have to tone it down because mi mouth too peppery.

Back On Board

So for you that say you cannot listen to certain types of music, stop lying to yourself.

I listen to Konshens. Oh Konshens keep your music clean because mi a listen to Caribbean Party and I have to get an ITunes Card and buy this song because I am flossing it if flossing is the right word. My youth, yu back inna mi good book again. Truly love Caribbean Party SO PEOPLE GET IT GET IT. Yes run out and buy the song on ITunes.

OTHER SONGS BY KONSHENS THAT I TRULY LIKE ARE:
- **A SUH MI TAN**
- **COUPLE UP**
- **NUH FALLA DEM(ADVICE TO THE YOUTHS)**
- **JAH NEVER LEAVE MY SIDE.** This song is so real because when you are trying and you achieve, wicked and evil people try to stop you; want bad things to happen to you).

Honourable Mentions

Delus   LOVE HATES YOU
Yes Delus yu sweet. Hence Duane Stephenson you have stiff competition for my heart. Buoy Delus you nice. A sweet eye candy. Buoy mi wi lust after you

any day. Hey mi caane look but mi caane touch because yu too young. Have to stay out of cougarville Jah noa.

Jah Vinci   **LIVE INNA FEAR**
                       NOBODY KNOWS *(WHERE DO ANGELS GO)*
                       CYAH WALK ALONE

Elephant Man   **DO THE RIGHT THING**
Buoy mi truly love Ben. Wow, Ben Jah noa.

Chi Ching Ching   **Way Up**
Laade mi call this one the stupid song and dance. People, only in Jamaica so WAY UP Chi Ching Ching because I truly love this song. It is infectious.

Don Husky   **BE GRATEFUL**
Tune mi youth, you have to be grateful for all hence your blessings come. Keep your blessings my youth, you will rise to the top truss mi on that.

Don Husky   **ON AND ON**
My youth it is hard when you are trying. Trust me I know the fight because the fight is not always physical, it is spiritual also.

Specialist, my youth wow because you guh haade fi real hence mi haffi mention yu. And people no matter how I cuss out my own, some sing the about the life they live. Yes the disrespect have to stop hence I saw the lady in Trench Town a discipline her son. Buoy she wap di boy good and proper because he lied and disrespected his elder. Yes some people a sey shi shouldn't slap di buoy suh, but respect goes a far. Respect lady because if dat was a ole time granny, tik pap up pan im. Truss mi mi ha some wrenking one. But mi lef dem to time. When mi nuh dey bout dem a guh feel it. Like I said retribution is a bitch when it hits you. As parents you can talk so much for the benefit of your children.

Oh it's April 24, 2015 and I forgot these. Closed my eyes and I saw this little white man. I would peg him to be about 5 feet tall if not a little taller but not taller than me. He was short. He had receding hair line and his hair was grey but paper white. He had round nose and he was dirty; filthy with white torn shirt on and light blue pants. Man the little devil would not let me forget his face because his face turned from pleasant to not so pleasant; hideous in my book.

Also saw this black man with dreadlocks. Pleasant looking face but he was in black clothing. His dreadlocks were so long but the weird part of his dreadlocks was the grey, beautiful grey streak he had going down one side; the left side. Simply beautiful.

Destruction dreams I am still having but I cannot fully remember them. All I can tell you is that I am still having them.

Oh dreamt Rob Ford was in my bed and we hadn't had sex in 6 months. I wanted to have sex but he couldn't, he just lay there. Yes I wanted to take it but didn't. All he said to me was that I was too noisy; loud. Nightmare or what. It's April 25th and this dream came through. My friend called me and I was talking really low……suffice it to say I was loud. Hence you know some blacks are whites and some whites are black. You see them in their original form in the spiritual realm. Get it now? If you don't, then I am sorry because I've done my best to educate you on the spiritual realm to certain degree. And for you who are wondering, he's black in the living (physical realm).

Dreamt about my friend. I was at my brother's place and my brother invited him. He was all smiles; happy to see me. It looked as if he cleaned himself up. So I sat on my brother's bed and pat the bed for him to sit beside me so that we could talk. Hence I am so going to watch this dream because this is a good sign I think. Yeah me, but the one thing I did not like was the injure mark he had in his head. Weird. And he was not in full black. I think he was in black pants but shirt was a mixture of white and light blue. But seriously, this dream is not for my White friend it's for my black friend. Hence the spirit world is throwing me for a loop and I truly don't know why?

I am being confused because I am in a confusing state when it comes to White People and what he Good God and Allelujah want me to say to them.

<u>Like I said, if you are clean in the living you have to start out with someone clean. You cannot start out with that person and or organization</u>

and or family unclean or you will become unclean; dirty.

It's like you have clean clothing on and you go into a sand storm and or dirty water. Your clothes and you will become dirty and it's not easy to clean your clothes; you. Sometimes your clothes do not come back clean and or come back to the original state of perfection. **So if you are clean lay with clean people not unclean people.**

And don't even go there because no Pastor on the face of this planet is clean. Absolutely none, hence you marry in filth and or dirt, baptize in filth and or dirt and die in filth and or dirt. I've told you in another book that if your Pastor is dirty, his sins fall on you because he presides over you.

DIRTY CAN ONLY MAKE CLEAN DIRTY; HENCE YOU CANNOT COMMUNE AND MARRY UNCLEAN PEOPLE. YOU WILL BECOME DIRTY AND OR UNCLEAN LIKE THEM. IF THAT PERSON NEED AND WANT TO BECOME CLEAN THEY MUST DO IT FOR SELF. A CLEAN PERSON IS NOT PERMITTED TO HELP THE UNCLEAN BECAUSE THEY WILL BECOME UNCLEAN ALSO. Yes there are certain things you can help with but you can only do so if the person requests your help. Meaning you cannot entertain a relationship with that person if he or she is unclean. It is forbidden. I know I am confusing you but this is the best explanation I can give.

In all that I've done in my life, I am learning and despite my feelings for him, he is forbidden to me because he's not on the road to truth. He talks the talk but he must now walk the walk.

Is it hard?

Yes but I truly don't want to be live Eve (Evening) and lose my place with Good God and Allelujah.

We say we love God but yet do all to hurt him; so we never truly loved him. Love is not truth because anyone can say they love you, and it's the ones that say they love you that screw up your life royally.

As humans we've become people of lies, hence we live in lies and some live for lies.

Many lie to bed you.

Many lie to take your soul and or spirit to hell with them.

Many lie and deceive you.

Many lie to you about Good God and Allelujah and I cannot do this because He Good God is my keep, and I refuse to lie for him and on him.

Many lie to you about Death and I cannot do this because Death did not come about like that. We created Death with our sins. Hence Death has a job to do and Death cannot stray from this.

THERE ARE TRUTHS AND THERE ARE LIES, AND IF YOU LIVE FOR LIES (SINS) YOU ARE GOING TO DIE. THERE ARE NO ANDS IFS OR BUTS ABOUT THIS.

TRUTH IS EVERLASTING LIFE, SO LIVE BY YOUR TRUTH AND GOODNESS AND LIVE COME ON NOW.

And no Kim, it matters not if you don't like the person. You don't like him hence this is your truth. Good God cannot sin you for not liking him or her. You went to him with your truth and there are no laws that say you have to like him or her.

If your truth is Satan it is Satan. Good God cannot sin you for worshiping Satan because this is your choice. Satan is your truth. However, do not expect him Good God to save you or continue to provide for you. If you are not a part of his true and good world, you will be left behind. Satan, who is your God, must save you in the end.

Don't go there because it's fair. There is a planet of death; hell, and this is where you must go. You did not choose life, you chose death. To conclude, like I said, I truly do not know what he Good God and Allelujah wants me to tell you the white race based on hue because I am at a confusing stage in my journey in regards to you the White Race. You cannot kill and expect someone to die for you, this is not right. Good God gave us all good and true life and we are the ones to reject him for someone else; other god and gods.

Death cannot change hence Death is white in hue; white in spirit, white all around, and death is YOU THE WHITE RACE.

So maybe, just maybe, Good God is trying to tell me that you are not going to be saved because of your wickedness. You cannot be saved just like that. <u>**AND LIKE I'VE SAID; IF I AM THE SAVING GRACE FOR HUMANITY I REFUSE TO SAVE ANYONE THAT IS WICKED AND EVIL.**</u> **HENCE LOOK AT YOUR PAST HISTORY AND ANCESTRY BECAUSE BILLIONS OF YOU WILL NEVER EVER BE SAVED BEYOND A SHADOW OF A DOUBT DUE TO THE WICKEDNESS YOU HAVE DONE AND YOUR HATRED AND VILE TREATMENT FOR BLACK PEOPLE AND YOUR OWN.**

Like I've said time and time again, truth cannot hate nor can truth kill. LIES HATE AND LIES DO KILL AND YOUR RACE BASED ON HUE AND ACCEPTANCE IS NOTHING BUT A BUNCH

OF LIARS AND THIEVES. YOU KILL BUT THEN AGAIN YOUR SKIN TONE REPRESENT DEATH ALL AROUND, SO YOUR MURDEROUS TENDENCIES SHOULD NOT SURPRISE ME. HENCE DEATH IS FOUND ON THE MOUNTAIN OF GOOD GOD AND ALLELUJAH. AS THERE IS LIFE THERE IS DEATH AND IT'S UP TO EACH AND EVERY HUMAN BEING TO LIVE LIFE GOOD, TRUE AND CLEAN AND BILLIONS CANNOT DO THIS HENCE DESTRUCTION COMES FOR MANY LANDS.

Remember we were told, *"THE EARTH IS THE LORD AND THE FULLNESS THERE OF AND ALL HE WHO DWELL THERE IN."*

So if the earth is the Lord and the earth is Female, why are we desecrating her like this?

Why do we rape and rob her of everything?

Why do we kill her and take life from her?

Good God gave her to us to maintain and sustain us and instead of cherishing her, we destroy her. So yes I am pleading to Good God and Allelujah for the final separation. **<u>GOOD AND EVIL MUST BE SEPARATED.</u>**

Good and evil must be separated in the flesh, in the spirit, in the universe; all around forever ever without end.

THE FINAL SEPARATION MUST COME SO THAT ALL IS WICKED AND EVIL; VILE AND SINFUL IS NO MORE INFINITELY AND INDEFINITELY FOREVER EVER WITHOUT END. I TRULY DO NOT WANT OR NEED ANYTHING THAT IS WICKED AND EVIL AROUND ME AND GOOD GOD AND HIS CHILDREN AND PEOPLE. I TRULY DO NOT WANT OR NEED EVIL; WICKED AND EVIL PEOPLE AND SPIRITS IN THIS WORLD ANYMORE. GOOD CANNOT COMMUNE WITH EVIL NOR CAN GOOD LIVE IN TRUE PEACE WITH EVIL. SO ALL FACETS OF WICKEDNESS AND EVIL; SIN MUST GO.

EVIL POLLUTES AND CONTAMINATE, AND THIS MUST STOP MORE THAN INDEFINITELY AND FOREVER EVER.

I AM PLEADING TO GOOD GOD AND ALLELUJAH TO NEVER EVER LET EVIL COME BACK ON EARTH EVER AGAIN FOR MORE THAN INFINITE AND INDEFINITE LIFETIMES AND GENERATIONS TO COME WITHOUT END.

I AM PLEADING WITH HIM FOR THIS (TO NEVER EVER LET EVIL COME BACK INTO THE UNIVERSE AND HIS GOOD AND TRUE PEOPLE) AGAIN FOR MORE THAN INFINITE AND INDEFINITE LIFETIMES AND GENERATIONS TO COME.

It is not good nor is it wise to have good and evil co-existing together. So as I continue to see his beautiful mountain, I am also asking for this infinite and indefinite more than forever ever without end banishment of death and all that is wicked and evil; sinful on his mountain as well. I am asking him to banish forever ever without end all facet (s) of sickness from his children and people also.

I am asking him with all that is good and true within me to eliminate the second level that has White People; Death. Death should not be on his mountain because he's seen the ways of death and it's not pretty. This is his mountain so no death; White People should not be on it based on hue. So for all that fall under the White

Banner of Death (whether Black, Chinese, Indian or White) access denied for more than infinite and indefinite lifetimes and generations more than forever ever without end to come. You are truly locked out, thus saith the Lord thy God meaning it is so. Good God, the Earth, the Good People of Earth, the Universe and Environment did not deserve the wickedness of man; humans. So if this is what he Good God want and need me to say to you as well as lock you out of his kingdom and abode, it is TRULY DONE. I DO SO IN HIS NAME WITHOUT REGRET AND PREJUDICE; HATE.

You cannot walk around and hate people and think there will not be consequences. There are consequences to our evil actions. So if this is the way to replenish earth and the universe as well as give Good God and Allelujah true peace and happiness; joy, then so be it. It is done because I more than truly love him unconditionally. He is my truth and I have to do all to save him despite my yoyo feelings of him sometimes.

And for all of you that say I cannot do this, yes I can just check the name of Good God and my name.

I fall under the banner of Judah; Life, hence Judah and or the children of Judah are not governed by the laws of men, they are governed by the law and laws of Good God and Allelujah. **Hence true life is kept through JUDAH AND NOT ISRAEL.**

We have to keep life and we have to maintain and sustain life for the good of all. If you go against good and true life, then you cannot be saved. You must die with the god of your choosing. **Billions of you did not accept life hence Billions of you cannot be saved.** So yes, the extinction of man – humans draw near and I will not change this. **Death knows the job he has to do and Death must do it, thus saith the Lord thy God meaning it is so.**

DEATH DOES NOT COME FOR THE RIGHTEOUS; DEATH COMES FOR ALL WHO ARE WICKED AND EVIL; SINFUL.

So now Lovey, as I close this book in truth, take Death and Sickness off your mountain because death is no longer needed on there. The time has come for evil to end, so truly end it and let your good and true people live in true peace and harmony with you. We must be void of all sin and evil; hatred. We must now live in true truth and happiness. No strife must we live in, hence good and true love must be our stay forever ever without end and that good and true love; stay is you and only you.

You are father and mother; hence we must truly love our one another truthfully in goodness and in truth. So yes death and sickness must be banished from off your mountains infinitely and indefinitely without end forever ever without end.

And for all of you that are saying I cannot banish the White Race, yes I can and I've done so. It is recorded and it must be so if I am the saving Grace for humanity and Good God and Allelujah.

<u>LIKE I'VE SAID IN MY OTHER BOOKS, EVIL DIE AS A WHITE PERSON DRESSED IN WHITE. WHITE IS DEATH IN THE PHYSICAL AND SPIRITUAL WORLD HENCE SATAN CAME TO EARTH TO DECEIVE HUMANS. Yes kill you. Death is in heaven and death is on earth. "As it is in heaven so it is on earth."</u>

Our skin tone represents life and death because the spirit is not a hue in its true form. Yes we are shown hue because this is all we know as humans. You do not know the spirit world hence you cannot speak of the spirit. I know it so I can speak of it. And there are no ands ifs are buts about this. There is a Black Death and there is a White Death **and I've told you GOOD GOD AND ALLELUJAH DOES NOT BASE ANYTHING ON HUE, HE BASE THEM ON THE GOOD AND EVILS THAT YOU DO.** Humans are the ones to base things on hue; the colour of skin and this is truly sad.

I'VE TOLD YOU NOT ALL WHITES ARE WHITE; FALL UNDER THE WHITE BANNER. MANY FALL UNDER THE BLACK BANNER WHICH IS THE BANNER OF GOD; GOOD GOD AND ALLELUJAH. I put things in the perspective of hue for you to comprehend not hate. All you know is hue, so knowledge must be given to you in hue and or based on hue.

I cannot hate you because your hue is White, I refuse to. I know the wickedness of every race on the face of this planet. **I'VE TOLD YOU WHEN WE SIN WE DIE, HENCE IT'S OUR SINS THAT KILL US. OUR SINS ARE OUR CURSE BECAUSE IT'S OUR SINS THAT TURN US WHITE; WHITE AS SNOW.**

So when you say you want to be white as snow, you are telling Him Good God and Allelujah you want to die; you want to become like death.

But the White Race is white. Pale. And stop because I've told you, WE ARE OF THE SAME GENE POOL, SO TRULY DO NOT GO THERE.

But they kill and bring forth sickness and death.
Every race does that due to sin.

But they kill and deceive.

Welcome to the real world of wicked and evil people; humans. YOU CANNOT BLAME THE WHITE RACE FOR DEATH BECAUSE IT WAS NOT THEM THAT INTRODUCED DEATH INTO THE EQUATION. IT WAS US THE SO CALLED BLACK RACE. Remember, the White race are not on the first level of Good God's Mountain, they are on the second level, the Black and Chinese race is on the first level, so if anyone is to blame it's the people on the first level who accepted sin; evil. And no we cannot blame this on the Ethiopians either because **Death existed long before Adam and Eve and the original Israelites.** Remember no Babylonian is on the Mountain of Good God, I never saw any. These are the fire people that many of our Black ancestors married and had children with. Hence many still speak the languages of Babylon until this day. And it matters not if you call the language Arabic, Sand script, Hebrew, Urdu, Farsi, English, Greek, Russian, Swahili or whatever. We accepted Babylon, the Children of Fire; Death; hence millions paid the price from then until this day. And yes I am so off track because it's April 26, 2015. Man I had some beautiful dreams. Dreamt the Blue Mountain and people this mountain is gorgeous. It's like 3 mountains were attached and it was green and beautiful with a couple dry patches here and there. But it matters not about the dry patches; the trees were gorgeous; truly beautiful. Hovering above the mountain was this red and silver helicopter with something and or a rope ladder hanging down from it. Wow. I was below the mountain in this chalet just taking in the scenery and this white lady asked me what is so nice and or great about the mountain and I gave her 3 answers. I told her the air and two other answers that had to do with the air and or the environment.

What a beautiful place but I cannot go up the Canadian Blue Mountain. I want to go up the Blue Mountain but I am forbidden to do so, and this is truly a bummer for me because I know the beauty of the Mountain of Good God and Allelujah. The Canadian Blue Mountain is not the mountain he Good God wants me to go up people.

Also dreamt my beautiful and gorgeous mother; yeah me because I am seeing her more and more.

The dream had to do with cakes, ice cream cakes and lots of them. Wow. My mother had some, meaning she got ice cream cake and in the dream and she was happy. And get this, she was pregnant. Weird because I've never seen a dead person pregnant before. Well I can't remember, but I am pretty sure I've never seen someone that is dead pregnant. So in your reading of these books let me know if I am incorrect or correct. You my gorgeous and beautiful family are my family of correction when it comes to errors in these books and or misquotes. Like I said, my mother was pregnant and I think she laid down and rings were at her head. She had this one particular bronze ring on and she took it off and threw it away and it landed in the sink. The ring she had on is like the fake bronze ring my last son is wearing. So I have to wonder if he or my first son got someone pregnant. Yes I know when you see old death it usually means new death but like I said, my mother was pregnant and this is so odd for me. **<u>As always if you know what these dreams mean please do not hesitate to let me know.</u>** I truly don't know if this means anything but I dreamt this tall light skinned man. I think he was deaf because he could not speak he could only write. He was writing something but I can't tell you what the writing said. His clothing of choice was light brown but not brown brown, but brown and or a tad lighter than paper brown.

Yes I dreamt about the WWE and a male dying.
Shaq dreamt about you but I can't fully remember the dream. Hence I must continue on my journey with Good God and hope that I have done what he's requested of me fully and truthfully.

Yes I need him and hopefully he continues to need me too. Yes I am thinking people because something truly does not make sense to me when it comes to the White Race based on hue. You the White Race base things off hue when it comes to people with Melanin. So when you continue to do this, how are you going to be saved? **<u>As far as I know, Good God has never ever sent anyone WHITE TO SAVE HUMANITY; HE'S ALWAYS SENT SOMEONE BLACK AND OR A MIXTURE OF RACE.</u>**

Jesus is White. **<u>Well according to your book of sin in revelations he's black; he has feet of burnt brass and nappy hair. NO WHITE MAN WOMAN OR CHILD HAS NAPPY HAIR APART FROM THE TRUE BLACK RACE.</u>** Yes go ahead and bring the science of hair into this so I can blast you and school your ass rude and proper. And trust me, I will take and or bring racism into this. So truly don't come here with your scientific bullshit and lies.

You base all on colour of skin, hence you keep telling people WHITE IS SUPERIOR TO ALL.

YOU KEEP SAYING YOUR HUE IS BETTER THAN EVERYONE ELSE; HENCE YOU HATE THE BLACK MAN WOMAN AND CHILD. YOU

DO ALL TO KILL THEM SO BECAUSE OF THIS, YOU BASING ALL ON HUE, COLOUR OF SKIN, GOD; GOOD GOD AND ALLELUJAH IS TELLING YOU POINT BLANK THAT YOU ARE ALL LOCKED OUT OF HIS KINGDOM AND IT MATTERS NOT IF YOU ARE GOOD OR EVIL. YOU LIVE FOR DEATH AND DO DREADFUL THINGS, HENCE THERE IS NO CHANCE IN HELL THAT ANY OF YOU WILL BE SAVED.

Keep your hue and White Supremacy bullshit; you are all locked out and rightfully so. Yes payback is a bitch NIGGAS. You've done too many vile and wicked things to others races, so truly weep and moan. Cry because Good God is truly not with you.

You're upset now aren't you?

Good because you do not hurt people and hate them without a cause. And even if you have a cause to hate someone, you do not hurt them. Live your life. You have a kingdom and land, it does not mean you have to entertain people that you do not desire to be in your land in your land. You truly do not like them, so if you truly don't like them do not live with or amongst them.

I don't want any Babylonians in my land and kingdom with Good God and Allelujah infinitely and indefinitely forever ever without end. I refuse all Babylonians hence petition Good God and Allelujah not to have any in our lands and kingdom. Yes you can call me racist, but I truly do not give a damn because **BABYLONS KINGS AND GODS INCLUDING QUEENS ARE NOT MY KINGS AND GODS, AND I TRULY DO NOT WANT ANY OF THEM TO COME INTO MY LAND AND LANDS WITH GOOD GOD AND ALLELUJAH AND POLLUTE IT.**

I do not bow down to idols, nor do I bow down to their gods anymore. (The Jesus bullshit people).

I know the truth of life and I have to live by the truth.

Don't come into my land and lands and condemn it hence the Mountains of Good God and Allelujah must truly remain clean.

And White People GOOD GOD WOULD NOT BE SO WICKED TO LOCK OUT ALL WHITE

PEOPLE. IF HE DID, HE WOULD BE LOCKING OUT A PART OF ME BECAUSE I HAVE WHITE BLOOD IN ME. HENCE MY TRUE ANCESTRY AND OR DESCENT. *Don't smile. Well yes smile because I would not be that wicked towards all of you. Some of you are good and truthful to black people though I truly do not know why. You all must have your reasoning for doing this. And no, I am not starting anything because I am truly confused when it comes to you. This is life I guess and so be it.*

Good God and Allelujah is with those who are with him; hence we have to put him first in all that we do.

Like I said, we are the ones that sin and fail him.
We are the ungrateful ones.
We are the ones to tell lies on him.
We are the ones to give him up for Death. So when Death come around to take you, then truly do not complain. You prayed (sinned) for death, hence Death must take you by any means necessary. (Malcolm X)

Michelle Jean

OTHER BOOKS BY MICHELLE JEAN

Blackman Redemption – The Fall of Michelle Jean
Blackman Redemption – After the Fall Apology
Blackman Redemption – World Cry – Christine Lewis
Blackman Redemption
Blackman Redemption – The Rise and Fall of Jamaica
Blackman Redemption – The War of Israel
Blackman Redemption – The Way I Speak to God
Blackman Redemption – A Little Talk With Man
Blackman Redemption – The Den of Thieves
Blackman Redemption – The Death of Jamaica
Blackman Redemption – Happy Mother's Day
Blackman Redemption – The Death of Faith
Blackman Redemption – The War of Religion
Blackman Redemption – The Death of Russia
Blackman Redemption – The Truth
Blackman Redemption – Spiritual War
Blackman Redemption – The Youths
Blackman Redemption – Black Man Where Is Your God?

The New Book of Life
The New Book of Life – A Cry For The Children
The New Book of Life – Judgement
The New Book of Life – Love Bound
The New Book of Life – Me
The New Book of Life – Life

Just One of Those Days
Book Two – Just One of Those Days
Just One of Those Days – Book Three The Way I Feel
Just One of Those Days – Book Four

The Days I Am Weak
Crazy Thoughts – My Book of Sin

MY TALK – BOOK FIVE

Broken
Ode to Mr. Dean Fraser

A Little Little Talk
A Little Little Talk – Book Two

Prayers
My Collective
A Little Talk/A Time For Fun and Play
Simple Poems
Behind The Scars
Songs of Praise And Love

Love Bound
Love Bound – Book Two

Dedication Unto My Kids
More Talk
Saving America From A Woman's Perspective
My Collective the Other Side of Me
My Collective the Dark Side of Me
A Blessed Day
Lose To Win
My Doubtful Days – Book One

My Little Talk With God
My Little Talk With God – Book Two

A Different Mood and World – Thinking

My Nagging Day
My Nagging Day – Book Two
Friday September 13, 2013
My True Love
It Would Be You

MY TALK – BOOK FIVE

My Day

A Little Advice – Talk
1313, 2032, 2132 – The End of Man
Tata

MICHELLE'S BOOK BLOG – BOOKS 1 – 20

My Problem Day
A Better Way
Stay – Adultery and the Weight of Sin – Cleanliness Message

Let's Talk
Lonely Days – Foundation
A Little Talk With Jamaica – As Long As I Live
Instructions For Death
My Lonely Thoughts
My Lonely Thoughts – Book Two
My Morning Talks – Prayers With God
What A Mess
My Little Book
A Little Word With You
My First Trip of 2015
Black Mother – Mama Africa
Islamic Thought
My California Trip January 2015
My True Devotion by Michelle – Michelle Jean
My Many Questions To God
My Talk
My Talk Book Two
My Talk Book Three – The Rise of Michelle Jean
My Talk Book Four